Seashore studies

PRACTICAL ECOLOGY SERIES

Seashore Studies
Urban Ecology
Grassland Studies

Series editor

Morton Jenkins, B.Sc., M.I.Biol.

Head of Science, Howardian High School, Cardiff
Chief examiner W.J.E.C. in CSE Biology
Examiner C.U.E.S.

PRACTICAL ECOLOGY SERIES

Seashore studies

Morton Jenkins, B.Sc., M.I.Biol.
Head of Science, Howardian High School, Cardiff

London
GEORGE ALLEN & UNWIN
Boston   Sydney

George Allen & Unwin (Publishers) Ltd,
40 Museum Street, London WC1A 1LU, UK

George Allen & Unwin (Publishers) Ltd,
Park Lane, Hemel Hempstead, Herts HP2 4TE, UK

Allen & Unwin Inc.,
9 Winchester Terrace, Winchester, Mass 01890, USA

George Allen & Unwin Australia Pty Ltd,
8 Napier Street, North Sydney, NSW 2060, Australia

First published in 1983

British Library Cataloguing in Publication Data

Jenkins, Morton
    Seashore studies.—(Practical ecology)
1. Seashore ecology—Great Britain
I. Title   II. Series
574.5'2638'094   QH541.5'S35
ISBN 0-04-574019-4

Library of Congress Cataloging in Publication Data

Jenkins, Morton.
    Seashore studies.
(Practical ecology, ISSN 0261-0493)
Bibliography: p.
Includes index.
1. Seashore ecology—Problems, exercises, etc.
2. Seashore ecology—Great Britain—Problems, exercises, etc.
I. Title. II. Series.
QH541.5.S35J46   1982   574.5'2638'076   82-16443
ISBN 0-04-574019-4

Phototypeset 10 on 12 point Times by D. P. Media Limited, Hitchin,
Hertfordshire
and printed in Great Britain by
Mackays of Chatham

Foreword

The aim of this series is to provide students and teachers of
Advanced level biological science with ideas for a practical
approach to ecology. Each book deals with a particular
ecosystem and has been written by an experienced teacher
who has had a particular interest in organising and teaching
field work. The texts include:

(a) an introduction to the ecosystem studied;
(b) keys necessary for the identification of organisms used
    in the practical work;
(c) background information relevant to field and laborat-
    ory studies;
(d) descriptions of methods and techniques used in the
    practical exercises;
(e) lists of materials needed for the practical work
    described;
(f) realistic suggestions for the amount of time necessary
    to complete each exercise;
(g) a series of questions to be answered with knowledge
    gained from an investigatory approach to the study;
(h) a bibliography for further reference.

Throughout the series emphasis is placed on *understanding*
the ecology, rather than on compiling lists, of organisms.
The identification of types, with the use of keys is intended
to be a means to an end rather than an end in itself.

Morton Jenkins
Series editor

Preface

The seven thousand miles of sea shore which surround
Britain are almost unique as a collection of truly natural
communities. Indeed, most littoral species which live on
British shores are the same as those which could have been
trampled by the Romans when they invaded us. The sea
shore is special because it is an area which is covered and
uncovered by salt water, twice a day in most parts of
Britain, and also in that it has the richest and widest variety
of organisms of all habitats available to students. The harsh
and continually fluctuating conditions in which littoral
organisms live have acted as selective pressures controlling
the evolution of these organisms. A practical study of their
ecology and behaviour can provide an opportunity to
reveal the secrets of their survival.

Morton Jenkins
December 1982

Acknowledgements

I am grateful to the Literary Executor of the late Sir Ronald
A. Fisher, FRS, to Dr Frank Yates, FRS and to Longman
Group Ltd, London for permission to reprint abridged
versions of Tables III, p. 46 and IV, p. 47 from their book
*Statistical tables for biological, agricultural and medical
research* (6th edn, 1974). I am also grateful to Mr D. E.
Rees for permission to reproduce Figures 7, 9, 14, 17, 18,
25, 26, 33 and 37. The quotation attributed to Charles
Elton at the beginning of Part A is taken from *The study of
ecology* by W. H. Dowdeswell and C. A. Sinker (Audio
Learning Ltd, 1977).

Contents

Introduction

For the purpose of the following practical investigations, the sea shore is defined as the zone between extreme high and extreme low tide marks. Areas of soil covered by high tide and uncovered at low tide are called salt marshes and are beyond the scope of this book.

As the limits of the investigations are defined by tidal range, it will be necessary to be familiar with the basic principles of the tidal phenomenon. The rhythmic movement of tides results in unique conditions on the sea shore. Organisms are subjected to water shortage for a period of hours and during this time are exposed to air, heat from the Sun, predation by birds, and sometimes temperatures below freezing point. At the time of high tide, aquatic conditions return and with them the problems of constant immersion in salt water.

The tides vary in time and range from day to day and also from place to place. Each day the time of high tide is approximately 50 min later than on the previous day, and since there are two high tides and two low tides every day in most parts of Britain, the interval between successive high or successive low tides is a little less than 12 h. The range of the tide varies on different days of the lunar month, being greatest immediately after a new or full Moon and least when the Moon is in the first or last quarter. Thus there will be a higher high tide and a lower low tide when there is a new or full Moon. Such a tide is called a spring tide. The slack tides of the first and last quarters are the neap tides. Tides of exceptional range occur near the March and September equinoxes, when the Sun and Moon exert maximum effect on the sea: these are called equinoctial spring tides.

Around our coast the shore may be rocky, sandy or muddy and each type is populated by a characteristic collection of plants and animals. Properties of water, such as temperature, salinity and proportion of dissolved gases, all play a part in determining the distribution of marine organisms. The physical effect of wave action is another very important factor which affects life on the sea shore.

Between tide marks there is a vertical zonation of plants and animals according to their degree of tolerance of desiccation at low tide. Each zone has a characteristic community, made up of four elements:

(a) the dominant species, few in number, which may give the community its name, e.g. the barnacle zone or lichen zone;

(b) the accompanying species, of which there may be many, none of which by itself forms a major part of the community, e.g. sand-hoppers among bladder wrack;

(c) the epifauna and epiflora of species living in company with the above, whether as parasites, commensals or encrusting growths, e.g. tube worms on sea weeds;

(d) the wandering fauna comprised of swimming or crawling animals, e.g. fish and large crustaceans.

In order to investigate the interrelations of organisms within these communities and the chemical and physical factors of the environment, it will be necessary to carry out work in both the field and the laboratory.

Keys

Background

> 'The aim of our science is to declare
> Why, and how much of what comes where.'
> Attributed to Charles Elton

It would be difficult to state the aim of ecology more concisely than this. The quotation attributed to Elton is a succinct description of the study of inter-relationships. It implies that the three most important questions to answer when studying an ecosystem are:

(a) What lives there?
(b) How many organisms live there?
(c) Why do they live there?

Ecologists find that knowledge of the natural history of the organisms living in a habitat is very useful and that the ability to identify these organisms is an essential prerequisite to answering questions (b) and (c).

The following keys are intended to help students wishing to identify the most common organisms of the sea shore. They are suitable for use in the field with the aid of a hand lens and basic biological knowledge, usually possessed by the interested naturalist. For more detailed identification see the bibliography (p. 83).

Key I: a preliminary identification key for common, free-living, multicellular animals of the sea shore

1 Bodies made of tissues firmly connected   Metazoa   **2**
    Spongy bodies loosely compact   (sponges) Phylum **Porifera**

These are impossible to identify to species in the field as the growth form of most species differs according to environmental conditions, e.g. exposure to wave action. Classification depends on the structure and composition of the spicules making up their skeletons.

2 Metazoa
Externally segmented, or with jointed legs, or in a tube, or in calcareous plates cemented to a solid substrate. **3**
Unsegmented. **10**
Fish-like. **15**

3 Worm-like, without *jointed* legs. May be in a tube.
Phylum Annelida, Class Polychaeta **4**
Jointed legs or calcareous plates. Phylum Arthropoda **6**

4 **Phylum Annelida, Class Polychaeta**
No obvious tube. Large parapodia (paddle-shaped legs).
Errant **Polychaeta**
In a tube. Sedentary Polychaeta **5**

5 **Sedentary Polychaeta**
Tube made of sand or gravel. No dorsal 'gills'. Family **Sabellidae**
Tube made of mucus and sand or gravel. Dorsal 'gills'.
Family **Terebellidae**
Tube made of calcium carbonate (white and stony).
Family **Serpulidae**

6 **Phylum Arthropoda**
Two pairs of antennae or in calcareous plates. Class Crustacea **7**
Six legs, one pair of antennae. Class Insecta **9**
Eight long legs, small bodies, spider-like. (sea spiders) **Pycnogonida**

7 **Class Crustacea**

> N.B. This preliminary identification of common sea shore animals excludes important planktonic groups of crustaceans, e.g. Copepoda, Mysidacea, Euphausiacea, Ostracoda. These are oceanic types and a microscope is necessary for their identification.

Bodies flattened dorso-ventrally like a woodlouse. Order **Isopoda**
In calcareous plates cemented to a solid substrate. Barnacles.
Order **Cirripedia**
Bodies flattened laterally like a sand-hopper. Order **Amphipoda**
Ten legs including at least one pair of pincers. Order Decapoda **8**

8 **Order Decapoda**
Short abdomen tucked under the cephalothorax (fused head–thorax). They walk sideways. (true crabs) Suborder **Brachyura**
Fairly short abdomen partially tucked under cephalothorax. May have abdomen in empty shell (hermit crabs). If not in empty shell, swim by flapping abdomen and cannot walk sideways, e.g. porcelain 'crabs' and squat lobsters. Suborder **Anomura**
Long abdomen not tucked under cephalothorax. Adapted for swimming with paddle-shaped appendages on the abdomen, e.g. prawns, shrimps, lobsters. Suborder **Macrura**

9 **Class Insecta** with no wings (the only true sea shore types).
Subclass **Apterygota**

10 Unsegmented with many tentacles surrounding the mouth. Mouth

and anus not separate. May be colonial, looking like miniature
fir trees.   Phylum Cnidaria (Coelenterata)   **11**

Unsegmented without tentacles. Worm-like.   Phylum **Nemertea**
Further classification depends on numbers of eyes present and the internal
arrangement of blood vessels.

Unsegmented with fleshy foot covered by dorsal visceral mass,
covered by sheet of tissue (the mantle). One or more shells may
be present.   Phylum Mollusca   **12**

Unsegmented, encrusting rocks or seaweeds.
May be plant-like in form. Colonial   Phylum **Bryozoa (Polyzoa)**
Difficult to distinguish from hydroid cnidarians (sea firs) in the field. Further
identification is only possible with a microscope.

Unsegmented. Star-shaped, spherical with spines or cucumber
shaped.   Phylum Echinodermata   **14**

Blob of jelly cemented to hard substrate or alga. Exhalent and
inhalent siphons (tubes) may be present.
                                    Subphylum **Urochordata (Tunicata)**
Tunicates are sometimes called sea squirts and may be solitary or colonial.
Further classification may require a microscope.

11   Phylum Cnidaria (Coelenterata)
Bodies exclusively solitary and polypoid (like a sea-anemone).
                                    (sea-anemones) Class **Anthozoa**

Bodies medusoid (like a jelly-fish) found stranded on the shore or
attached to seaweeds.   (jelly fish) Class **Scyphozoa**

Bodies colonial and polypoid. Plant like in shape. Polyps are very
small in horny cups or at the end of long stalks.
                                    (sea firs) Class **Hydrozoa**

12   Phylum Mollusca
Eight dorsal shell plates.   (chitons) Class **Polyplacophora**
Two shell valves   Class **Bivalvia**
With one shell or without an external shell.
Foot not divided into tentacles.   Class Gastropoda   **13**
Foot divided into eight or ten tentacles.
                                    (cuttle fish and octopus) Class **Cephalopoda**

13   Class Gastropoda
One external shell. With operculum or cone shaped.
                                    Subclass **Prosobranchiata**
No external shell.   Subclass **Opisthobranchiata**

14   Phylum Echinodermata
Star-shaped. No marked division between body and arms.
                                    (star fish) Class **Asteroidea**
Spherical.   (sea urchins) Class **Echinoidea**
Small central disc with five long arms which drop off easily.
                                    (brittle stars) Class **Ophiuroidea**
Cucumber shaped.   (sea cucumbers) Class **Holothuroidea**
Central disc with branched arms.   (feather stars) Class **Crinoidea**

15   Vertebrates with paired fins and biting jaws.   (fish) Class **Pisces**

Key 2: a key to the most common British molluscs normally included in a transect of a rocky shore

1	With a conical shell.	**2**
	With a spirally-coiled shell.	**3**
2	**Limpets** (see Fig. 1)	
	Orange foot.	***Patella aspera***
	Grey–green foot. Transparent marginal tentacles. The most common limpet on the shore.	(common limpet) ***Patella vulgata***
	Grey–green foot. White marginal tentacles. Only found in the south-west.	***Patella depressa***
	Shell with eight to ten iridescent blue stripes. Only found on lower shore.	(blue rayed limpet) ***Patina pellucida***
3	Shell with a groove near the aperture. A carnivore, feeding mainly on barnacles and mussels	(dog whelk) ***Nucella lapillus***
	Shell without groove near the aperture.	**4**
4	Mother-of-pearl in aperture.	(topshells) *Trochidae* **5**
	No mother-of-pearl lustre in aperture.	(winkles) *Littorinidae* **6**

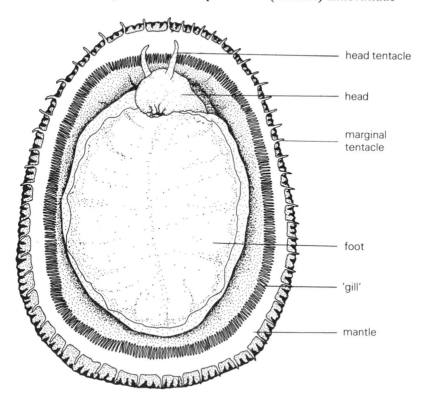

head tentacle

head

marginal tentacle

foot

'gill'

mantle

Figure I A ventral view of *Patella vulgata*. To be used with the key to *Patella* spp.

5 Trochidae

Dark purple stripes on a purple background. Large hole (umbilicus) near aperture. Middle-shore in pools. Only found in south and west of Britain.   (purple top shell) *Gibbula umbilicalis*

Greyish-purple. No marked striations. Tooth-shaped lump on inner edge of aperture. Middle-shore. Only in Ireland, South and West Wales, Devon and Cornwall.

(toothed top shell) *Monodonta lineata*

Narrow grey stripes on light grey or fawn background. No well marked hole (umbilicus) near aperture. Lower shore.

(grey top shell) *Gibbula cineraria*

Attractive, blotched bright pink or light purple. May be white. Very pointed. Only on lowest part of shore.

(painted top shell) *Calliostoma zizyphinum*

6 Littorinidae

Very small (up to 5 mm long). Surface bloom like a black grape. Splash zone. Exposed shores. Often in empty barnacle cases. Beware of confusion with young rough winkles.

(nerite winkle) *Littorina neritoides*

Small (up to 10 mm long). Ovo-viviparous. Young ones aggregate in crevices and empty barnacle cases. Easily confused with nerite winkle but do *not* have surface bloom. Rough surface. Lip of aperture meets main shell at an angle of 90°. Colour variable. Most common on upper shore but will extend to lower shore.

(rough winkle) *Littorina saxatilis*

No spire. Colour variable. Middle shore with wracks.

(flat winkle) *Littorina littoralis**

With obvious spire (up to 20 mm long). They aggregate under rocks on middle shore. Young ones can be confused with adult rough winkles but lip of aperture meets main shell at an angle of less than 90° and there is a white patch near aperture.

(edible winkle) *Littorina littorea*

---

* In 1967, Sacchi and Rastelli subdivided *L. littoralis* into two species, namely, *L. obtusata* (L.) and *L. mariae* Sacchi and Rastelli. The latter is smaller and is only distinguishable from the former by the more extended tip to its penis. According to Moyse it occurs lower down the shore than *L. obtusata* (L.). They are impossible to tell apart in the field using external features.

Key 3: a simple key for the identification of the *most common and most widely distributed* British seaweeds

N.B. *This key is designed for the student of ecology rather than for the student of phycology. Those interested in the details of individual species should consult the references listed in the bibliography.*

1   Green.   2
     Brown.   4
     Red.   9
2   Membranous, like thin lettuce leaf.   (sea lettuce) ***Ulva lactuca***
     Tubular, unbranched thalli.   ***Enteromorpha* spp.**
     Thread-like thalli.   3
3   Unbranched. Spine on tip of thallus (hog's bristle)***Chaetomorpha* spp.**
     Branched. Very dark green tufts (50 mm).   ***Cladophora* spp.**
     Feather-shaped. Very delicate. In pools on lower shore.
                                                              ***Bryopsis* spp.**
4   Thin, tubular, unbranched. Only in south and west.
                                                           ***Asperococcus* spp.**
     More widely distributed.   ***Scytsosiphon* spp.**
     Shapeless gelatinous, sponge-like masses (to 30 mm diameter).
                                                              ***Leathesia* spp.**
     Fine threads, often epiphytic.   one of the **Ectocarpales**
     Strap-shaped, many branches.   5
     Large, leathery, broad straps with a large stalk and holdfast (up to
        3 m long). Not branched.   8
5   With air bladders.   6
     Without air bladders.   7
6   Paired bladders. Forms zone on middle shore.
                                            (bladder wrack) ***Fucus vesiculosus***
     Single, egg-shaped bladders (*not paired*). Forms zone on middle
        shore. Often with epiphytic tufts of the red *Polysiphonia* spp.
                                     (egg or knotted wrack) ***Ascophyllum nodosum***
     Small, pod-shaped, oval bladders on tips of branches. In pools,
        often with brown tufts of epiphytic *Sphacelaria* spp.
                                          (pod weed) ***Halydris siliquosa***
7   Small branched straps (up to 150 mm long × 5 mm wide). Inrolled
        margin to thalli. In splash zone. Black and brittle when dry.
                                       (channelled wrack) ***Pelvetia canaliculata***
     Flat thalli (up to 200 mm long). Sometimes spirally twisted.
     Spherical, gelatinous, reproductive bodies on tips of thalli.
     Forms zone on upper shore just below channelled wrack.
                                          (spiral or flat wrack) ***Fucus spiralis***
     Thalli with serrated edges. Forms zone on lower shore.
                                          (serrated or saw wrack) ***Fucus serratus***

Thong-shaped thalli. Branched, growing from toadstool-shaped
base. On lower exposed shores.   (thong weed) *Himanthalia* **spp.**
Delicate thalli obviously dichotomously branched. End divisions
blunt. Olive brown.   *Dictyota dichotoma*

8 Large divided thalli (up to 2 m long). Large stalk and holdfast.
May form zone on lower shore.
(kelp) *Laminaria digitata* or *L. Hyperborea*
Undivided thallus, crinkly (up to 3 m long).   *Laminaria saccharina*
Undivided thallus with midrib. Only on lower shore of very
exposed areas.   (marlins) *Alaria* **spp.**
Flattened, wavy stalk. Massive, hollow, warty holdfast. Thallus up
to 2 m long. Lower shore only.   *Saccorhiza polyschides*

9 Pink encrustation. White when bleached by sun. Limy. Middle
shore pools and below.   *Lithothamnion* **spp.** or *Lithophyllum* **spp.**
Leaf shape. With midrib and 'veins'. Lower shore only.
Delessaria **spp.** or *Phycodrys* **spp.**
Broad, flat, thin thallus.   **10**
Narrow, flat, thallus.   **11**
Filamentous, thread-like.   **14**
Round in TS, gelatinous. Often branched.   **15**
Segmented thallus.   **16**
Feather shaped thallus.   **17**

10 Very thin thallus. Purple or black. Occurs as a slimy, membranous
film on exposed rocks   (laver) *Porphyra* **spp.**
Quite tough. Pink. Translucent. Very variable in shape. Branched.
Disc holdfast (thallus up to 300 mm long). Lower shore, sometimes epiphytic, e.g on *Laminaria* spp.
(dulse) *Palmeria* (*Rhodymenu*) **spp**
Very tough. Dark red. Opaque. Crisp to bite. Lower shore.
(pepper dulse) *Dilsea* **spp.**

11 With midrib.   **12**
Without midrib.   **13**

12 Sharply pointed dichotomous branches. Delicate. Only in south
and west.   *Hypoglossum* **spp.**
Blunt, rounded, dichotomous branches. Delicate.
Apoglossum **spp.** or *Membranoptera* **spp.**

13 Marked dichotomy (up to 80 mm long). Blue tinge, almost iridescent under water. In pools on middle and lower shore.
(carragheen or Irish 'moss') *Chondrus crispus*
Marked dichotomy (up to 100 mm long). Inrolled thallus forming
channel. Usually dotted with pustular reproductive bodies. On
exposed shores.   *Gigartina stellata*

14 Branched tufts. Often epiphytic on *Ascophyllum* spp. *Polysiphonia* **spp.**
Fine, delicate, pink filaments. Much branched. Hooked tips to
thalli.   *Ceramium* **spp.**

Very coarse, wiry texture. Almost black. *Ahnfeltia* **spp.**
15 Very slimy. May show dichotomy. Dark purple. Summer annual.
In pools. *Nemalion* **spp.**
Stiff, rod-like, branched thalli. Claw-shaped holdfast.*Furcellaria* **spp.**
Stiff, rod-like, branched thalli. Disc-shaped holdfast. *Polyides* **spp.**
Limp, fairly broad, main thallus. Disc holdfast. Branches become
narrow at points of origin. *Dumontia* **spp.**
16 Multi-branched. Very coarse limy segments. Pink but may be
white. In pools rich in lime. (coral weed) *Corallina* **spp.**
Multi-branched. Very soft segments. Lower shore only.
Lomentaria **spp.**
17 Soft and limp. Feather-shaped often with the purse sponge on it
(*Grantia* **spp.**). Lower shore only. *Plumularia* **spp.**
Branched like Christmas tree. Almost brown. Middle and lower
shore. Variable in length. *Laurencia* **spp.**

Key 4: a key to the most common genera of invertebrates living in British sand and mud

---

1 Externally segmented or with jointed legs or in tube. 2
Unsegmented. 27
2 Worm-like without jointed legs. May be in tube.
Phylum Annelida 3
With jointed legs. Phylum Arthropoda 10
3 **Phylum Annelida**
Living in tube. 4
Not in tube. 7
4 Large tube from 20–50 cm long by 1 cm wide. 5
Long fine tube up to 20 cm long by 0.3 cm wide. 6
Delicate conical tube of pure sand carried on worm. *Pectinaria* **spp.**
5 Leathery tube with no attached gravel. *Sabella* **spp.**
Gravel attached to tube. Fringe of sand at end. *Lanice* **spp.**
Gravel attached to tube. No fringe of sand at end.
Branchiomma **spp.**
6 Up to 10 cm long. Head with branched 'gills' poking out of tube.
Gravel attached to tube. Yellowish-green body. *Owenia* **spp.**
Very fine tube. Up to 20 cm long by 1 mm wide. Tube made of silt
and mucus. No gravel attached. Very delicate worm with bright
red dorsal blood vessel. *Pygospio* **spp.**
7 Without parapodia (swimming paddles). 8
With parapodia. 9
8 Body like an earthworm with a dilated anterior and tufts of 'gills'.
No tentacles on head. *Arenicola* **spp.**
Body with orange head tentacles and thread-like 'gills'.*Amphitrite* **spp.**

9 Fleshy parapodia. Head with fleshy tentacles and eversible jaws.
Dorsal red blood vessel. Buried in mud.   *Nereis diversicolor*
Small parapodia. Head without fleshy tentacles. Whitish-grey
body. Moves rapidly like snake when disturbed.   *Nephthys* **spp.**
Iridescent bristles on back and on parapodia. Massive oval body.
10–20 cm long. Found only on lower shore.   *Aphrodite aculeata*

10   Phylum Arthropoda
Two pairs of antennae.   Class Crustacea   **11**
With wings.   Class **Insecta**

These are mainly temporary visitors to the shore as opportunist feeders and are
beyond the scope of this key. Some Diptera lay eggs in the strand line. Cole-
optera and Hemiptera are common, particularly in the vicinity of salt marshes.

11   Class Crustacea
Woodlouse-shaped (flattened dorso-ventrally).   **12**
Sand-hopper-shaped (flattened laterally).   **13**
With ten legs including pincers.   Order Decapoda   **24**

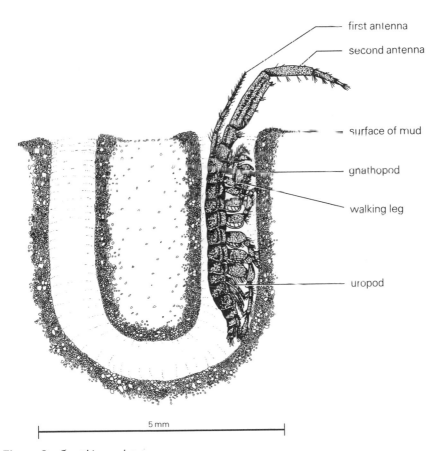

Figure 2 *Corophium volutator.*

12 In mud, often swimming in pools.   *Sphaeroma* **spp.**
    In mixture of sand and mud or in pure sand.   *Eurydice* **spp.**
13 In strand line.   **14**
    In sand.   **23**
    In mud. 8 mm long. Second antenna half as long as body. In
      permanent U-shaped burrow 1 cm below mud (see Fig. 2).
                                                   Corophium volutator
14 **Sand-hoppers** (see Fig. 3)
    Jumping animals. Walk and stand upright. First antenna much
      shorter than second and without a branch. Extreme tip of tail
      and last pair of appendages not divided into two.   Talitridae **15**
    Typically wriggling on their sides. First antenna longer than sec-
      ond and having a small branch. Extreme tip of tail and last three
      pairs of appendages all divided into two.   Gammaridae **16**
15 **Talitridae** (see Figs 4a and b)
    Smooth edges to joints of second pair of antennae. First antennae
      hardly ready to last joint of second pair, with spines on upper
      edge.   *Orchestia* **spp.**
    Rough edges to small joints at end of second antennae. Appen-
      dages from second segment behind head end in a spike; from
      third segment end in a small claw. Very common near salt
      marshes.   *Talitrus saltator*
16 **Gammaridae**
    Spines on last three segments of abdomen and tail.   **17**
    No spines on last three segments of abdomen and tail.   *Melita* **spp.**
17 Inner branch of last pair of appendages (third uropod) less than
      half the length of outer branch.   *Marinogammarus* **spp.**
    Inner branch of last pair of appendages more than half the length
      of outer branch.   **18**

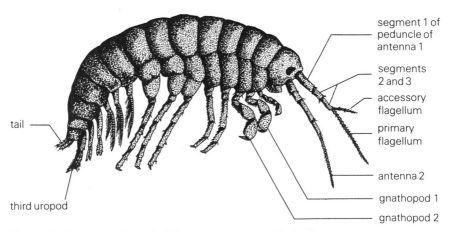

Figure 3 Diagram of a typical *Gammarus* for use with the key.

(a)

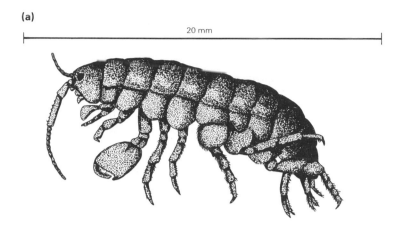

20 mm

(b)

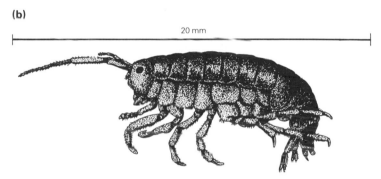

20 mm

Figure 4   (a) *Orchestia gammarella*; (b) *Talitrus saltator*.

18 Hand of gnathopod 1 smaller than hand of gnathopod 2; primary
flagellum has 34 or more joints and accessory flagellum has
more than seven.   **19**

Hand of gnathopod 1 is about the same size as hand of gnathopod
2; primary flagellum has fewer than 34 joints and accessory
flagellum fewer than seven.   **21**

19 Segment 1 of peduncle of antenna 1 is about as long as segments 2
and 3 of antenna 1 combined; accessory flagellum has 8–14
joints. Antenna 2 has 24 joints (see Fig. 5).   ***Gammarus locusta***

Segment 1 of peduncle of antenna 1 is only slightly more than half
as long as segments 2 and 3 combined; accessory flagellum has
7–9 joints. Antenna 2 has 15 joints.   **20**

20   Appendages, tail and antennae with dense, long hairs and setae.
Gammarus zaddachii zaddachii
Appendages, tail and antennae with few, short setae.
G. zaddachii salinus
21   Small eyes: flagellum of antenna 2 has 13 segments.
Gammarus pulex
Large eyes: flagellum of antenna 2 has less than 10 segments.   **22**
22   Antenna 2 is almost as long as antenna 1; the fourth and fifth
segments of antenna 2 are about the same length as one another.
Gammarus duebeni
Antenna 2 is much shorter than antenna 1 (2 : 3); fifth segment of
antenna 2 is shorter than fourth.   *Gammarus chevreuxi*
23   4 mm long, translucent, red eyes. First antenna arises from a horn
(see Fig. 6a).   *Bathyporeia* **spp.**
6 mm long, yellowish-orange. First antenna does not arise from a
horn (see Fig. 6b).   *Urothoë* **spp.**
8 mm long, sandy colour. Minute eyes (hardly visible) (see
Fig. 6c).   *Haustorius* **spp.**
24   **Order Decapoda**
Abdomen extended like a prawn.   **25**
Abdomen tucked under cephalothorax like a crab.   **26**
25   Spike on head. In muddy pools near salt marshes.
Palaemonetes varians
Without spike on head. On sand. May be buried.   *Crangon vulgaris*
26   On mud near salt marshes and estuaries. On sand only where rocks
present. Typical crab shape. Greenish.   *Carcinus maenas*
Buried in sand on lower shore. Anterior long 'schnorkle'.
Corystes **spp.**

25 mm

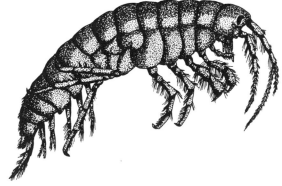

Figure 5   *Gammarus locusta.*

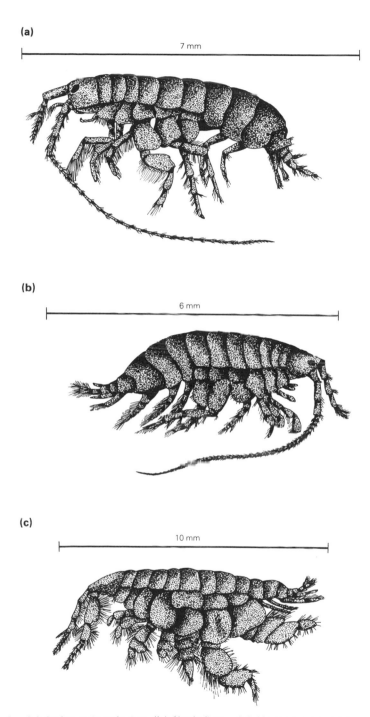

(a)

7 mm

(b)

6 mm

(c)

10 mm

Figure 6   (a) *Bathyporeia pelagica*; (b) *Urothoë* sp.; (c) *Haustorius arenarius*.

27 Tentacles arranged radially.   **28**
    Tentacles not so arranged.   **29**

28 Sea anemones
    Base attached to rock or shell buried in muddy sand.   *Cereus* **spp.**
    Base not attached. Buried in sand.   *Peachia* **spp.**

29 Worm-like   Phylum **Nemertea**
     Further identification depends on numbers of eyes and their arrangement on the
     head. A microscope is necessary for this. The most common are *Lineus ruber*
     and *Tetrastemma* spp. in mud. *Cerebratulus* spp. is flattened dorso-ventrally and
     is found in sand only on the lower shore.
    Not worm-like.   **30**

30 With shells (one or more) or looks like a slug.   **31**
    Star-shaped or spherical with spines.   Phylum Echinodermata **39**

31 One shell.   **32**
    Two shells.   **33**
    Slug-like without a shell.   Nudibranchia **38**

32 On mud, up to 6 mm long. May be buried. (Any larger snail on
    mud is probably a winkle. See p. 5.)   *Hydrobia ulvae*
    On mud, up to 10 mm long. Delicate, translucent shell with
    flattened spire. May be buried.   *Retusa* **spp.**
    On sand on lower shore. Massive shell up to 200 mm long. With
    horny operculum.   *Buccinum undatum*
    In sand only on lower shore. Foot and mantle cover shell. Shell
    50 mm long, shiny.   *Natica* **spp.**

33 In pure, viscous mud.   **34**
    In sand or sandy mud.   **35**

34 6.25 cm long. White–brownish. Oval. *Flattened*. Buried up to
    20 cm.   *Scrobicularia plana*
    2.5 cm long. *Globular*. Pink, white or purple. Often banded.
    Interior of shell pink or purple. Buried up to 5 cm.
                                            Macoma balthica

35 Up to 3 cm long. Fine, saw-like margin to shell.   *Donax vittatus*
    Length roughly same as breadth.   **36**
    Length longer than breadth.   **37**

36 Up to 4.5 cm long, thick triangular, horizontal ribs. Whitish or
    cream, sometimes with brown markings.   *Venus striatula*
    Up to 5.0 cm long, a crenulated margin. Vertical ribs, brownish
    white.   (common cockle) *Cerastoderma edule*
    Up to 5.0 cm long. Very smooth, triangular. Brownish pink.
                                            Mactra corallina
    Up to 6.5 cm long. Roundish and cream coloured.   *Tellina crassa*
    Up to 10.0 cm long. Globular. Very spiny. Vertical ribs. Crenu-
    lated margin.   (spiny cockle) *Acanthocardia aculeata*
    Up to 12.5 cm long. Massive black shell.   *Cyprina islandica*

37   Up to 2.0 cm long. Triangular. Yellow-orange-pink. Thin.
   Tellina tenuis

   Up to 12.5 cm long. Brownish with peeling outer coat. Lower
   shore only.   *Lutraria lutraria*

   Up to 15.0 cm long. Rather triangular. Brownish white. Burrowing in mud with long siphon.   *Mya arenaria*

   Up to 20 cm long. Very narrow compared to length (ratio 6 : 1).
   Razor shells. Lower shore only.   *Ensis* **spp.**

38   **Nudibranchia**

   Up to 6 mm long. Smooth. Found feeding on algae (*Vaucheria*
   spp.) on mud.   *Limupontia depressa*

   Up to 10 mm long. Dorsal surface with protrusions (cerata) on
   mud.   *Alderia modesta*

39   **Phylum Echinodermata**

   Star-shaped.   **40**

   Spherical. The burrowing sea urchin. Found in sand on lower
   shore.   *Echinocardium cordatum*

40   A perfect star in sand on the lower shore.   *Astropecten irregularis*

   Small central disc with long delicate arms. Brittle stars. Burrowing
   in sand on lower shore.   *Acrocnida brachiata*

   Those washed up on the surface of the sand are likely to be *Ophiura spp.* or
   Ophiocomina spp.

Zonation

Background
(Refer to Introduction, p. xi.)

Animals and plants are never scattered haphazardly over the shore. They are often confined to one of five zones which are called:

(a) the splash zone;
(b) the upper shore;
(c) the middle shore;
(d) the lower shore;
(e) the sublittoral fringe.

The splash zone is only covered by extremely high tides, whereas the sublittoral fringe is uncovered only at corresponding extremely low tides. The major factors which influence zonation are:

(1) Tidal range (see Introduction p. xi)
Shores with little tidal range possess very little zonation.
(2) The time of low water of spring tides
The different times of day at which low water of spring tides occurs influence the conditions prevailing on the lowest part of the shore, e.g. on the south coast of Devon and Cornwall the low water of spring tides uncovers the lower shore at midday, whereas in the Firth of Clyde and the Irish Sea coasts, the same levels are uncovered at 18.00 h when the Sun has less of an effect. Species which are absent on the lower shore in Devon and Cornwall may be able to survive in the Firth of Clyde because they suffer less insolation.
(3) Exposure to wave action
Certain organisms are unable to exist on very exposed shores but are abundant on sheltered ones, whereas others favour exposed conditions and find it impossible to compete successfully on sheltered shores. The degree of wave action also affects the widths of zones.
(4) The slope of the shore
There is a direct relationship between the slope of the shore and the widths of zones.
(5) Desiccation
There is a graded resistance to drying and other effects of insolation shown

by sea shore organisms. Those of the upper shore have more adaptations for resisting desiccation than those of the lower shore.

(6) Selective settlement of larvae

Certain organisms have some means of controlling their initial settlement on the shore. Barnacle larvae select regions which have been occupied by adults of the same species. Similar selection occurs by the larvae of tube worms.

(7) Competition for food and space

The limits of the zones of many algae are controlled by herbivores and carnivores have a similar effect upon the zones occupied by encrusting animals. Different species of brown algae compete for space within the same zone as do the encrusting red algae with barnacles and tube worms.

(8) Kineses and taxes

Many invertebrates maintain their zones as a result of kinetic and tactic mechanisms related to humidity. They often aggregate in crevices within their normal zones.

(9) Seasonal variation

Certain mobile animals alter their positions on the shore according to seasonal variations of temperature. The zones of maximum abundance of such species will therefore depend on the time of the year.

Exercise 1: to investigate a pattern of zonation on a rocky shore

One way of determining the distribution of animals and plants is to use the technique of a belt transect.

Materials

A graduated pole, a metre rule and a split level; 60-m tape measure or a length of rope marked at intervals of one metre; chalk; a quadrat (½ m²); tide tables; identification keys for molluscs and algae (see pp. 4 & 6); note-book pencil, graph paper.

Time

At least 3 h in the field and 2 h in the laboratory.

Method

Ideally, three people should work as a team; two for making the profile and one for recording the data.

Consult a reliable table of tides for the area to ascertain (a) the time of low tide and (b) the predicted level of low tide relative to Chart Datum. (Chart Datum is an arbitrary zero, reached only rarely by the tide.) The most favourable time to carry out a belt transect is when the tide is receding at a spring or autumn equinox.

Choose a rocky shore having as regular a slope as possible with a dense covering of algae.

The exercise is divided into three parts:

(a) the construction of the profile of the slope of the shore;
(b) the determination of the frequency and the distribution of species with the aid of the quadrat;
(c) the recording and analysing of data.

(a)   The construction of the profile of the slope of the shore
Begin at the top of the shore. Make a clear chalk mark near the last of the terrestrial plants (Station 0). Lay the rope or tape along the shore, at right angles to Station 0, pointing towards the sea. This procedure ensures that you follow the most direct course to the sea. Secure both ends of the rope or tape. Place one end of a metre rule on the chalk mark and, keeping the rule horizontal (use a spirit level), point it towards the sea at right angles to Station 0. Hold the graduated pole vertically at the end of the rule, opposite Station 0. Station 1 is where the bottom of the pole rests on the shore. The difference in height between Station 0 and Station 1 can now be measured on the graduated pole.

Place the metre rule at Station 1 and proceed as before to obtain a reading for the level of Station 2 below Station 1. Continue at 1 m intervals in a seaward direction. The data for the profile can be recorded in the field as follows:

Station	Level below previous station (m)	Total drop (m)	Substrate
0	0	0	bed rock
1	X	X	bed rock
2	Y	$X + Y$	bed rock
3	Z	$X + Y + Z$	pebbles

A rise in the substrate is considered as a negative drop when read off the pole at the *preceding* station.

Try to reach the bottom of the shore, i.e. your last station, at exactly the predicted time of low tide. The level of this station above or below Chart Datum can be noted by reference to the tide tables and must be added to, or subtracted from, the last total drop reading to give the actual level of Station 0 above Chart Datum.

(b)   The determination of the frequency and the distribution of species with the aid of a quadrat
Lay your quadrat on the last station, horizontally (Fig. 7), and count the *living* animals and *attached* plants in the ½ m² area. Continue at suitable

Figure 7 Students using a quadrat while carrying out a belt transect of a rocky shore (photo courtesy of D. E. Rees).

intervals to Station 0. (The intervals will depend on the total length of the shore uncovered at low tide, which will depend on the slope.) On a very flat shore make your counts every 3 m. Hurry, because the tide is now chasing you. Sparsely distributed animals can be counted individually. The numbers of dense encrusting types, e.g. barnacles and tube worms, can be expressed in terms of percentage cover or estimated using abundance scales (see p. 24). Plant numbers can be expressed in terms of percentage cover (Fig. 8). Thus, if there was nothing but bladder wrack in 50 per cent of the quadrat, the results would show 50 per cent bladder wrack and 50 per cent bare rock. Any material which cannot be identified on the shore should be collected for future identification in the laboratory. *A single specimen, adequately labelled, is sufficient and this should be returned to the shore to avoid destruction of the environment.*

Questions

Using your observations and background reading (p. 16), answer the following:

(1) Which organisms appeared to be dominant in the

  (a) splash zone,
  (b) upper shore,
  (c) middle shore,
  (d) lower shore?

Profile

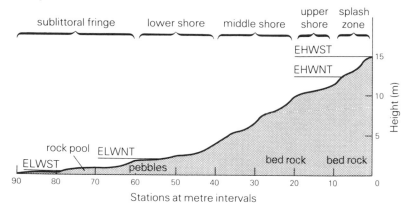

Examples of histograms

Fucus vesiculosus
10 vertical squares
= 100% cover

Littorina littoralis
10 vertical squares
= 20 individuals

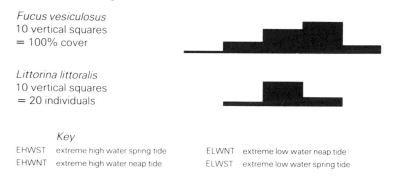

Key

EHWST	extreme high water spring tide	ELWNT	extreme low water neap tide
EHWNT	extreme high water neap tide	ELWST	extreme low water spring tide

Figure 8   How to express data illustrating a belt transect.

(2)   Which organisms accompanied the dominant types in the above zones?

(3)   Give an example of (a) an epiphyte and (b) an epizoite which you found on the shore.

(4)   Organisms of the splash zone spend up to 80 per cent of the year out of water. Relate this fact to

(a)   the shape of channelled wrack (Fig. 9);

(b)   kineses and taxes shown by many invertebrates living in the splash zone;

(c)   the modifications of the 'gill' of the small nerite winkle to form a 'lung';

(d)   uric acid is the main nitrogenous excretory product of the nerite winkle;

(e)   the nerite winkle can respire anaerobically for short periods.

Figure 9 The channelled wrack, *Pelvetia canaliculata*, at low tide (photo courtesy of D. E. Rees).

(5) Relate the ovo-viviparity and internal fertilisation of the rough winkle to its normal zone on the shore (i.e. the zone where you found it to be most abundant).

(6) The *adult* wracks of the middle shore are not eaten by the winkles which occur there. Winkles are not carnivorous. Suggest three sources of food for winkles, found in the same zone.

(7) Explain your observations concerning the abundance and variety of life on the lower shore compared with the upper shore.

(8) Suggest (a) a herbivore which can control the limits of the bladder wrack, (b) a carnivore which can control the limits of barnacles, and (c) two encrusting animals which compete for space with an encrusting red alga. (See p. 75 for feeding habits.)

(9) Examine specimens of the following carefully and suggest how they resist desiccation at low tide:

    (a) winkles;
    (b) limpets;
    (c) barnacles;
    (d) tube worms.

(10) Suggest a mechanism to explain how barnacles and tube worms settle from the plankton near the adults.

Exercise 2: to investigate the effects of different exposures to wave action on zonation

Background

For the purpose of this investigation, exposure to wave action is defined as the amount of physical buffeting that an organism receives as a result of the movement of water on the shore, and includes the abrasive effects of tidal streams running over rocks.

Wave action on the shore varies greatly even over small distances. Some shores are almost land-locked, so sheltered that no waves larger than ripples ever reach them, while others are buffeted on most days by large rollers or the breaking swell from storms far out at sea. Every kind of intermediate condition exists between these extremes.

A scale which could measure the relative exposure of shores to wave action would be very useful to an ecologist as a frame of reference within which shores can be compared. It is not necessary that the scale should be an exact or direct measure of wave action, provided it allows biological data to be related in an orderly and understandable way.

Biological measurements made of the abundance and levels of growth of the common, shore-dwelling organisms could be used as a basis for the scale. This scale would be closely related to the amount of wave action, although not a precise measure of it. Different species growing on rocky shores require different degrees of protection from certain aspects of the physical environment, of which wave action is often the most important. They can survive and flourish in different degrees of exposure to these forces. Thus, the following scale is an exposure scale in the broad, everyday sense of the word. It attempts to give the shore ecologist an idea of the abundance of certain indicator species which may be used to determine the degree of exposure of a particular shore.

In Britain, the most exposed shores are generally those facing the prevailing south west winds, although local conditions of the immediate surroundings may provide some degree of protection.

Subjective terms used to describe the abundance of species can be changed to a more quantitative form as follows:

Key: +++ abundant; ++ common; + present.

Barnacles
+++ = more than 1 per cm²; rocks well covered.
++ = 0.1 to 1 per cm²; up to ⅓ of the rock covered.
+ = 10 to 100 per m²; few within 10 cm of each other.

Limpets
+++ = more than 50 per m².
++ = 10 to 50 per m².
+ = less than 10 per m².

A biologically defined exposure scale

A summary of species which indicate degrees of exposure

Indicator species	Extremely exposed	Very exposed	Exposed	Semi-exposed	Fairly sheltered	Sheltered	Very sheltered	Extremely sheltered
Alaria esculenta (marlins)	+++	++	–	–	–	–	–	–
Himanthalia elongata (thong weed)	+++	+	–	–	–	–	–	–
Porphyra umbilicalis (laver)	+++	+	–	–	–	–	–	–
Gigartina stellata	+++	+++	+++	–	–	–	–	–
Fucus vesiculosus evesiculosus*	+++	+++	+++	+	–	–	–	–
Lichina pygmaea (blacklichen)	+++	+++	+++	+	+	–	–	–
Patella aspera (limpet)	+++	+++	++	++	+	+	–	–
P. depressa (limpet)	+	+++	++	+	+	+	–	–
Chthamalus stellatus (southern barnacle)	+++	+++	+++	++	++	+	–	–
Littorina neritoides (nerite wirkle)	+++	+++	+++	++	+	+	–	–
Supra littoral lichens	+++	+++	+++	+	+	+	+	–
Lithothamnion/Corallina (coral weed)	+++	+++	+	+	+	+	+	+
Semibalanus balanoides (acorn barnacle)	++	+++	+++	+++	+++	+++	++	+
Patella vulgata (common limpet)		+++	+++	+++	+++	+++	+++	+
Littorina saxatilis (rough winkle)	++	+++	+++	++	+	+	+	+
Nucela lapillus (dog whelk)	++	+++	++	++	++	++	+	+
Mytilus edulis (mussel)	++	+++	+	++	+	+	+	+
Laminaria digitata (kelp)	–	+++	+	++	++	++	+	+
Fucus serratus (serrated wrack)	–	+	++	++	+++	+++	+++	+++
Pelvetia canaliculata (channelled wrack)	–	+	+	++	++	+++	+++	+++
Gibbula umbilicalis (purple top shell)	–	–	+	++	++	+++	+++	+++
Fucus vesiculosus (bladder wrack)	–	–	–	+	–	+	+++	+–
F. spiralis (spiral wrack)	–	–	–	+	+	++	+++	+++
Ascophyllum nodosum (knotted wrack)	–	–	–	–	+	++	+++	++
Laminaria saccharina (kelp)	–	–	–	–	+	++	+++	+++
Littorina littorea (edible winkle)	–	–	–	–	+	++	++	+++
L. littoralis (flat winkle)	–	–	–	++	++	++	+++	+++
Monodonta lineata (toothed top shell)	–	–	–	+	++	++	++	+++

Key: +++ abundant; ++ common; + present; – absent.

* This is bladder wrack without bladders

Top shells and the dog whelk
+++   = more than 10 per m².
++   = 1 to 10 per m².
+   = less than 1 per m².

Nerite winkles and rough winkles
+++   = more than 1 per cm².
++   = 0.1 to 1 per cm².
+   = very few in crevices.

Flat winkles and edible winkles
+++   = more than 50 per m².
++   = up to 50 per m².
+   = less than 1 per m².

Mussels
+++   = more than 20 per cent cover.
++   = large patches up to 20 per cent cover.
+   = scattered individuals.

Lichens
+++   = more than 20 per cent cover.
++   = up to 20 per cent cover.
+   = widely scattered patches.

Algae
+++   = more than 20 per cent cover.
++   = less than 20 per cent cover.
+   = scattered individuals.

The aims of the investigation are:

(a) to compare an exposed shore with a sheltered shore in terms of zonation;
(b) to try to classify types of shore based on the biologically defined exposure scale (p. 23).

Materials

Same as those for a belt transect (p. 17) plus the biologically defined exposure scale (p. 23).

Time

At least 3 h per transect.

Method

Carry out a transect of each selected shore using the method described on p. 17. In order to select an exposed or sheltered shore, use the biologically defined exposure scale and identify indicator species living on the shore.

Questions

(1) Compare the slopes of the shores studied. Relate the slope to the abundance of indicator species.
(2) Relate the differences in the widths of the zones of organisms, on different shores, to the varying degrees of exposure experienced on these shores. Explain your observations of the upper shore and splash zone.
(3) Suggest why *Littorina neritoides* does not occur on very sheltered shores but can exist on very exposed shores.
(4) By reference to the shore(s) that you have studied, suggest factors other than exposure which could determine the presence or absence of the indicator species in the biologically defined exposure scale.
(5) Discuss the limitations of the use of a biologically defined exposure scale.

Exercise 3: to investigate the effects of wave action on the bladder wrack, *Fucus vesiculosus*

Background

Wave action is one of the most important factors which control the shapes of many of the flora and fauna of rocky shores. On extremely exposed shores, a bladderless variety of *Fucus vesiculosus*, called *Fucus vesiculosus* var. *linearis* (*evesiculosus*), is recognised by phycologists. On such shores there appears to be little survival value in having air bladders to aid floatation for photosynthesis. Flora and fauna survive the constant battering action of waves and have a characteristic shape related to wave action, e.g. stunted mussels and dog whelks. Between the two extremes of very sheltered and very exposed shores lies a series of variation. (See p. 23 for exposure scales.)

The features to be investigated in *Fucus vesiculosus* are:

(a) length of thalli;
(b) degree of branching;
(c) number of bladders per unit length (in *F. vesiculosus* bladder formation occurs each April);
(d) thickness of stipe (the stalk of the seaweed);
(e) diameter of the holdfast.

Materials

Metre rule; calipers; exposure scale (p. 23).

Time

3 h.

Method

Select at least three sites which vary in respect of their exposure to wave action. The three sites should be at the middle shore level and at least 50 individuals from each shore must be used for measurements. Select one factor at a time and use the Student–*t* test for comparison of the variables (see p. 86).

Record the abundance of indicator species for the shores used in the investigation. This will give you an idea of the degree of exposure to which the sites are subjected.

Questions

(1) Discuss the value of using *F. vesiculosus* var. *linearis* as an indicator species for estimating the degree of exposure of a shore to wave action.
(2) Construct your own exposure scale for the shores used in the exercise.

Biomass and feeding interrelations

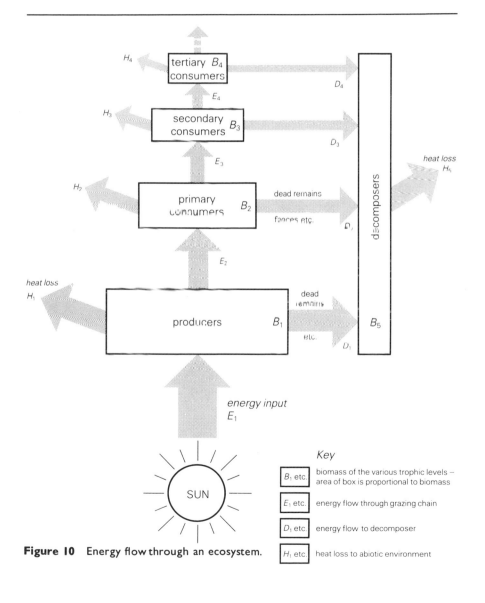

Figure 10 Energy flow through an ecosystem.

Key

B_1 etc.	biomass of the various trophic levels – area of box is proportional to biomass
E_1 etc.	energy flow through grazing chain
D_1 etc.	energy flow to decomposer
H_1 etc.	heat loss to abiotic environment

Background

The energy that all heterotrophic organisms derive from their food can always be traced back to plants where, initially, it was captured in photosynthesis. The energy that is stored in plants can be passed to a herbivore, then to a carnivore and lastly to a saprophyte. This type of energy supply relationship, which may link six or more organisms, is called a food chain. The first link in any food chain is always a green plant or detritus, part of which is the dead remains of plants. These plants are sometimes described as producers. The next link in the chain, called a primary consumer, is usually a herbivore (some are omnivores). A carnivore, the secondary consumer, makes up the third link, while in some cases, other carnivores occupy additional levels. Each link in the chain can be called a trophic level.

In the following investigations we will be interested in the total amount of

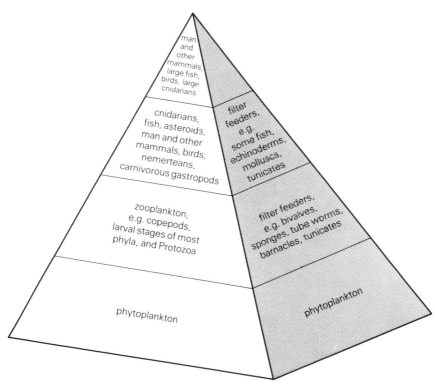

Figure 11 A theoretical biomass pyramid for a sea shore with phytoplankton as the producer.

living matter existing at each trophic level. The total mass of living matter is referred to as the biomass. Estimates of biomass allow meaningful comparisons of different ecosystems to be made and pyramids of biomass to be constructed.

By no means all of the stored chemical energy present in the producer is appropriated by the primary consumer. It has been estimated that, in some cases, as little as 0.1 per cent of the chemical energy stored in plants is converted into available energy in the primary consumer. A similar wastage occurs between subsequent stages of the food chain. The biomass of the animal population within a community is related to the plant biomass. This is illustrated in Figure 10. Such pyramids for the shore are shown in Figures 11, 12 and 13 but in practice quantitative measurements of biomass are often different to the theoretical model.

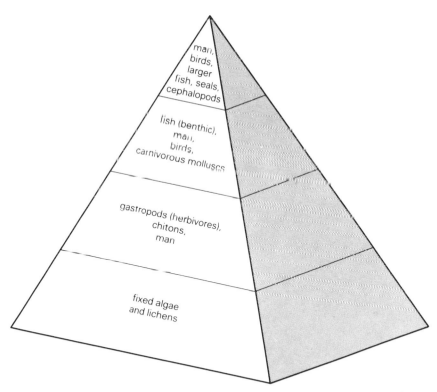

Figure 12 A theoretical biomass pyramid for a sea shore with fixed plants as producers.

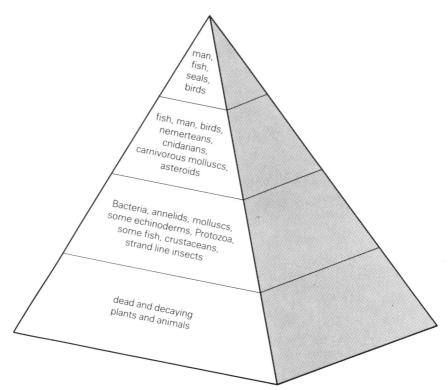

Figure 13 A theoretical biomass pyramid for the sea shore with detritus as the producer.

Exercise 4: the construction of a biomass pyramid using a standing crop of algae

N.B. *Any study of biomass which involves clearing areas of organisms should be limited to a very few groups of students, or second-hand data may be used for a discussion. The conservation of the environment is essential and repeated clearance on the same shore might lead to depletion of certain species.*

Materials

A quadrat (½ m²); a trowel; a spring balance.

Time

1 h on the shore; 1 h in the laboratory.

Method

Select a shore with a dense covering of algae (see Fig. 14). Place a ½ m²
quadrat on the standing crop of a selected species. Collect all the living
animals present in the quadrat. Sort them into primary and secondary
consumers. (See p. 75 for information on feeding.) Consider detritus feeders and scavengers as primary consumers. Weigh each group. Cut every
plant in the quadrat at the base of its holdfast. Carefully hand sort the algae
for attached animals. The animals must be weighed and included in your
data for primary and secondary consumers. Weigh the algae using the spring
balance. Return all the material to the shore.

In the laboratory, express the weights on graph paper in g m⁻². The
weights will include water content and exoskeletons. Take values for at least
three separate quadrats and obtain a mean value for each level of the
pyramid. Express your results graphically as shown in Figure 15.

Figure 14 A rocky shore which is well covered with a mixed population of the
co-dominant species *Fucus vesiculosus* and *Ascophyllum nodosum* (photo courtesy of
D. E. Rees).

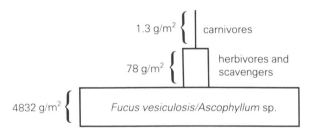

Figure 15 Results obtained with a standing crop of fucoid algae as the producer.

Exercise 5: the construction of a biomass pyramid for a filter-feeding community, e.g. a mussel bed

Materials

A quadrat (½ m²); a spring balance.

Time

1 h on the shore; 1 h in the laboratory.

Method

The method is basically the same as that used for a region with a standing crop of algae. The main difference is that instead of completely clearing a given area and weighing the organisms directly, an estimate of the biomass of mussels and attached barnacles is made. Ecologically, mussels and barnacles are similar in their filter feeding role within an ecosystem. Take ten mussels of a representative size for the mussel bed and calculate the weight of a single mussel (with barnacles still attached). Count the number of similar sized mussels and barnacles within an area of ½ m² using the quadrat horizontally. The biomass of mussels and barnacles per m² can then be

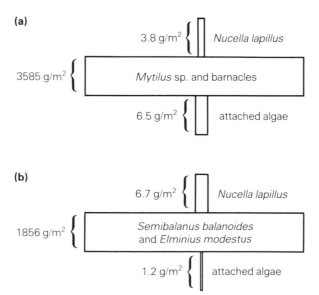

Figure 16 (a) The pyramid of biomass resulting from an ecological analysis of a mussel bed; (b) the pyramid of biomass similarly obtained for a region densely covered by barnacles.

estimated. Collect the other animals within a typical ½ m², sort them into primary or secondary consumers (see p. 75) and weigh them. If there is any attached alga within your sampling area, collect it and weigh it.

You are interested in relative biomass rather than absolute biomass so that you can compare producer and consumer levels. Record your data graphically as shown in Figure 16a and b. *Return all material to the shore. Even dead organisms can be eaten by others within the ecosystem.*

Questions

(1)   Give reasons why crabs and dog whelks are invariably under-sampled.
(2)   Explain the relatively enormous biomass of algae compared with the biomass of herbivorous molluscs within the same area.
(3)   What are the producers on a mussel bed?
(4)   Suggest two methods of estimating their abundance.
(5)   Explain why any method of estimating the biomass of producers on a mussel bed will be an under-estimation of their productivity.

Rock pools

Background

Rock pools provide fluctuating environmental conditions which test the adaptability of their inhabitants. Changes in temperature, salinity and pH have to be tolerated. Large pools on the lower shore exhibit less variation than small shallow pools of the upper shore, which may not receive sea water for several consecutive days or even weeks. Diurnal and nocturnal changes in the physical and chemical characteristics can be measured quantitatively and can be related to the position of the particular pools on the shore. Similarly, biotic factors of pools may be detected by comparing the differences in species composition at different levels and analysing the requirements of these varying populations.

Exercise 6: an investigation of the biotic and abiotic factors of an upper, a middle and a lower shore rock pool

Aims

(1) to compare the biotic and abiotic factors of the pools;
(2) to determine the fluctuation of salinity, oxygen, pH and temperature over a period of 24 h in a rock pool.

Materials

Tape measure; metre rule; thermometer; oxygen meter; pH meter; conductivity meter (or see below for laboratory method of determining chloride concentration); identification keys (see pp. 1–6); graph paper.

Time

Aim 1 (above) 3 h; aim 2 (above) 24 h.

Method

Select three pools; one on the upper shore, one on the middle shore and one on the lower shore. The pools should not be too deep or too large because the purpose of the investigation is to compare the environments of each pool, and it will be necessary to identify all the macroscopic inhabitants. Make a map of the pools carefully to scale, indicating the dimensions (see Fig. 17), shape and depth at various points. Each organism present in the pool must be noted on the map in its natural position. The plants should be represented by shaded areas, the animals should be indicated as individuals. A comparison of the flora and fauna from each pool must then be made and the types present should be related to the physical and chemical factors within their environments, e.g. oxygen, pH, temperature and conductivity (salinity).

Ideally, to achieve the second aim (above), the chemical and physical factors should be measured hourly over a period of 24 h, for a single pool. Temperature can be measured directly with a field thermometer. In order to measure the oxygen concentration of each pool, readings relative to oxygen saturated water can be made with an oxygen meter. It is far simpler to use than the archaic Winkler titration method, which is designed for laboratory use, and includes toxic chemicals dangerous in field situations. Plot a graph of the oxygen concentration against (a) time and (b) temperature.

Figure 17 Students measuring a rock pool for the purpose of constructing a map (photo courtesy of D. E. Rees).

It is possible to use pH test papers for estimating the hydrogen ion concentration although the accuracy obtained is seldom greater than 0.3 pH units. It is important to regulate the size of the sample drop so that the spread on the test paper is not too great – approximately 0.5 cm in diameter.

A much more accurate estimation of pH is possible with direct readings of a pH meter. Many portable field models are available, and, as with the oxygen meter, enable investigations to be carried out throughout a 24 h period.

Direct measurement of salinity poses an unsolved problem to the ecologist. Quantab 1177 chloride titration papers (obtainable from Philip Harris Biological Ltd) are convenient measuring devices, calibrated to give quantitative estimations of chloride ions in aqueous solutions. Each titrator consists of an inert plastic strip in which is fixed a capillary tube impregnated with silver dichromate. The lower end of the capillary tube is placed in the solution to be tested and becomes filled by capillary attraction. When saturated, the length of white silver chloride in the capillary is measured against a numbered scale on the strip. Chloride concentration is obtained by equating it with the scale reading using a calibration table provided with each bottle of titrators.

The titrators operate by making use of the reaction of chloride ions with silver dichromate:

$$Ag_2Cr_2O_7 + 2NaCl \rightarrow Na_2Cr_2O_7 + 2AgCl$$

(brown)   (white)

Obtain a small sample of sea water to be tested in a narrow specimen tube (not more than a depth of 0.5 cm). Dip the strip into the sample and take the reading on the scale after the yellow strip at the top of the column has turned dark blue. This takes about 12 min. The result must be read between 30 s and 5 min after the blue colour appears. Convert the Quantab reading into percentage sodium chloride, or parts per million of chloride ions, or the total salinity as given below:

Quantab reading	p.p.m.Cl (mg Cl l^{-1})	NaCl (per cent)	Total salinity (per cent)
3.4	9 100	1.5	15
4.1	12 000	2.0	20
4.6	14 800	2.5	25
5.1	17 900	3.0	30
5.55	21 100	3.5	35
5.85	24 500	4.0	40
6.2	27 100	4.5	45

After recording all measurable changes graphically discuss the effects of the physical and chemical changes on pool populations.

Questions

(1) Make a list of the organisms found in the pools studied.
(2) Explain the changes that you have observed over a 24 h period in (a) oxygen concentration, (b) pH, (c) salinity.
(3) Explain the sharp boundary between barnacles on the outside of the pools and encrusting red algae on the inside.
(4) Which of the following are present both in and out of the pools: (a) nerite winkle, (b) dog whelk, (c) limpet, (d) flat winkle, (e) mussel?
(5) From your observations on lower shore pools, explain the presence of normally sublittoral (deep water) animals and plants.

Limpets

Exercise 7: an investigation of the homing instinct of limpets

Background

The homing behaviour of limpets has interested naturalists for many years. An investigation of the phenomenon is relatively easy to carry out in the field, but the interpretation of the observations is more difficult. When feeding, the limpet moves from its 'home' to graze on the surrounding algal sporelings and afterwards returns to *exactly* the same position. Eventually the shell may become worn so as to fit the rock, or vice versa (see Fig. 18). The ecological significance of this behaviour is that limpets can maintain their positions in the most favourable zones.

Figure 18 Limpets cling so firmly that they erode the rock substrate (photo courtesy of D. E. Rees).

Materials

Nail varnish *or* ICI Belco 300 paint; pen knife; tape measure.

Time

At least 24 h.

Method

Choose a population of limpets on as smooth a shore as possible. Outline the bases of 30 common limpets with nail varnish or ICI Belco 300 paint (which can be painted directly on to wet surfaces). Paint a number on the shell of each limpet and number each 'home' so that it corresponds to the number of its occupant. Dislodge the limpets *very carefully* with a pen knife *so that the shells are not damaged in any way*. Place the limpets at a measured distance (no more than 3 m) from their original homes. Check their positions 24 h later. If several groups of students have carried out the investigation, use all the data and apply the Chi-squared test to test the null hypothesis that the limpets' return was due to pure chance.

Example

Five samples of 30 limpets, A, B, C, D and E were collected. The individuals of each sample had their bases outlined in a particular colour of nail varnish. Each 'home' was numbered and so was the occupant's shell. The numbers returning after a full tidal cycle were recorded. Fewer limpets from sample B returned than from the other samples. Was this a result of pure chance? Apply the Chi-squared test as follows:

Formula

$$\chi^2 \text{ (Chi squared)} = \Sigma \frac{(O-E)^2}{E}$$

Where O = the number *observed* to have returned;
E = the number *expected* to have returned.

Results

	Groups					Totals
	A	B	C	D	E	
observed O	23	7	25	19	21	95
expected E	19	19	19	19	19	95
$(O-E)$ deviation	4	−12	6	0	2	0
$(O-E)^2$	16	144	36	0	4	
$\dfrac{(O-E)^2}{E}$	0.842	7.579	1.894	0	0.211	$10.526 = \chi^2$

One needs a null hypothesis to give a series of expected results, E, with which to compare the observed results, O. We wish to find out if Group B is at a disadvantage in returning to their homes so a suitable null hypothesis is that there is *no difference* in the chances of their returning. If this is true, the expectation is that an equal number of limpets will return from each group. The total number returning was 95 limpets so, for equality, there should be 19 returning from each group.

There are four degrees of freedom $(n - 1)$, where n is the number of categories (Groups A to E in this case). From the results above, $\chi^2 = 10.526$ when P (the probability) is between 0.05 and 0.02 (see p. 88). If the null hypothesis is true, one would expect deviations as big as these in only 2–5 per cent of instances. Thus evidence is strongly against the null hypothesis and it must be discarded. There is a 95–98 per cent chance that the differences in the numbers returning really are significant. It seems that Group B was at a disadvantage and an explanation other than chance must be looked for.

Questions

(1) Suggest reasons why there was not 100 per cent return.
(2) Suggest possible mechanisms to explain the homing instinct.
(3) Devise experiments to support your hypotheses.

Exercise 8: to investigate any relationships between the shell shapes of limpets and exposure to wave action

Background

The exposure to wave action of a shore can be estimated by referring to the biologically defined exposure scale (see p. 23). The ratio of the base diameter and the height of the shell is used to demonstrate a quantitative relationship between the shape of the shell and exposure to wave action.

Materials

Calipers; ruler; spirit level.

Time

The period of low tide on two or more days.

Method

Select a sheltered and an exposed shore. Measure the base diameter and height of 50 limpets from each shore at the middle shore level. Use calipers to measure the diameter and use a ruler and spirit level to measure the height of the shell (see Fig. 19).

Plot the measurements of the base diameter against the height for the samples taken from each shore.

The dog whelk is another animal whose shell shape varies according to the degree of wave action it withstands. Similar comparisons can be made with this species by measuring the length of the shell and the width of the aperture. In this case the length can be plotted against the aperture width. There is less chance of damaging dog whelks than limpets because dog whelks can be dislodged without reducing their chances of survival.

Questions

(1) Is there any difference between the graphs for exposed and sheltered shores?

(2) (For the mathematically inclined) if the graphs are very similar, find out if there is a statistically significant difference between the base : height ratios of the samples by using the Student-t test. (See p. 86 for method and p. 89 for tables.)

(3) Explain the advantages to the limpets of any relationships which you have observed when you compared samples from sheltered and exposed shores.

(4) Why could measurements from randomly collected empty shells not be used for this investigation?

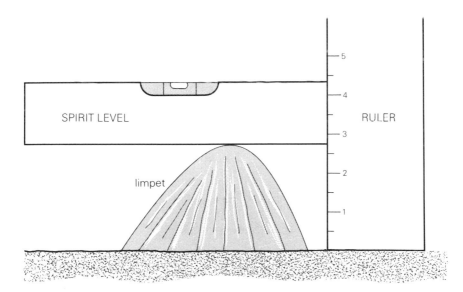

Figure 19 Measurement of the height of a limpet.

Exercise 9: an estimation of the age of a population of limpets

Background

The common limpet has a reproductive period lasting for a short time during each year. By measuring the size of individuals within a sample area you can obtain the frequency of various classes of sizes. The ecological significance of this exercise is apparent when one needs to investigate the rate of recolonisation of an area which has been subjected to abnormal conditions, e.g. a particularly harsh winter or the effects of pollution.

Materials

Calipers; ruler.

Time

At least 3 h.

Method

Select a shore with a dense population of limpets. Measure the diameters of 100 specimens using calipers. Be careful to include very small ones which may be 1 mm in diameter. Plot the data in the form of a frequency diagram (numbers against size classes).

Questions

(1) What is the total number of peaks on your frequency distribution?
(2) What does this figure represent?

Barnacles

Exercise 10: an investigation of the success of the immigration of the Australasian barnacle, *Elminius modestus*

Background

During World War II, the Australasian barnacle (see Fig. 20a) became established on British shores. It was first recorded near Southampton in 1943 and can now be found as far north as the Firth of Forth. The increase in shipping between the northern and southern hemispheres during the war years probably aided the invasion of our shores by this barnacle.

(a)

(b)

(c)

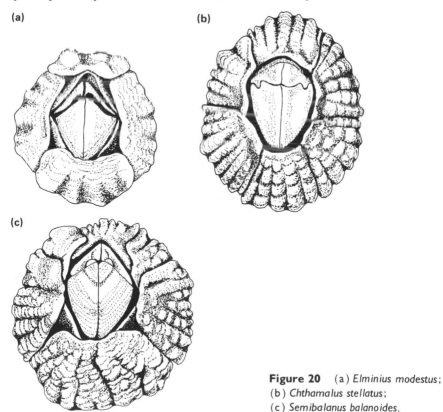

Figure 20 (a) *Elminius modestus*;
(b) *Chthamalus stellatus*;
(c) *Semibalanus balanoides*.

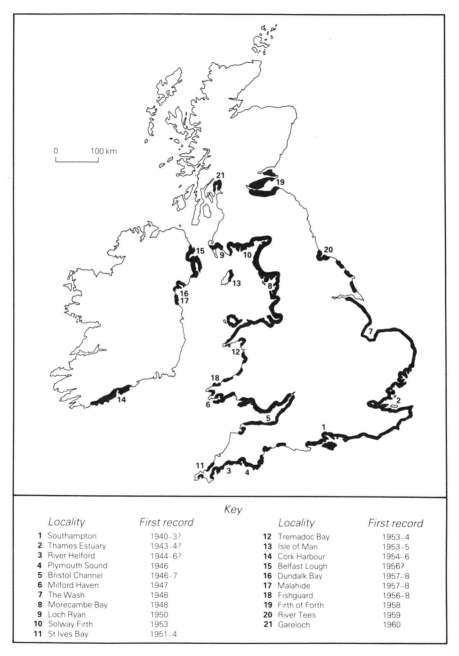

Figure 21 Map showing, in heavy outline, the areas in which *Elminius modestus* can be found in Britain, together with a list of localities and their probable date of colonisation. The areas of colonisation and the probable order in which they have been established are given by the numbers.

Materials

Quadrat.

Time

At least 1 h.

Method

The relative abundance of the three most common species of barnacles found in Britain can be estimated by random throws with a ½ m² quadrat on shores which are subject to varying degrees of wave action. Even experts find it difficult to identify certain adult barnacles in the field and there can be

Figure 22 Map showing, in heavy outline, the distribution of *Semibalanus balanoides* around Britain. This barnacle is an arctic species, with a southern limit of distribution in north-west Spain.

much confusion between *Semibalanus balanoides* and *Chthamalus stellatus* based on external features (see Figs 20a, b and c). Wave action can distort their normal shapes. *Elminius modestus* can easily be identified because of its four shell plates. The other two species mentioned both have six shell

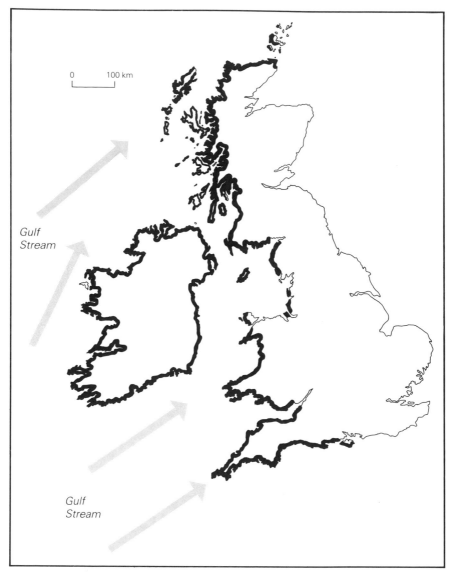

Figure 23   Map showing, in heavy outline, the distribution of *Chthamalus stellatus* around Britain. This barnacle is a southern species and its distribution around Britain is influenced by the Gulf Stream.

plates. The establishment of *Elminius* sp. in an area can be compared with that of other species by estimating their percentage frequency in a large number of random quadrats.

Questions

(1) *Elminius* has a higher tolerance of low salinity than the two native barnacles found in a similar zone. Where is the invader most likely to be successful?

(2) *Elminius* shows the following differences compared to the native species:

    (a) it can withstand lower temperatures than *Chthamalus*;

    (b) it can withstand higher temperatures and more desiccation than *Semibalanus balanoides*;

    (c) it has a higher feeding rate and growth rate than either of the native species.

Use these facts to explain the spread of *Elminius* sp. as shown on the map (Figs 21, 22 and 23).

(3) Suggest how the spread of *Elminius* sp. around Britain has been achieved.

Exercise 11: an investigation of the predation on barnacles by dog whelks

Figure 24 Dog whelks, with their egg cases, among barnacles. (Note that some of the barnacles do not have opercular plates.)

Background 1 (see Fig. 24)

The predation habits of dog whelks on barnacles can be investigated by counting the number of barnacles which have been attacked by dog whelks in a given area and comparing them with the number of dog whelks present.

Materials	*Time*
Quadrat.	1 h.

Method

Select an area with a dense covering of barnacles where dog whelks are present. Place the quadrat horizontally on the area and count

(a) the number of living barnacles,
(b) the number of dead barnacles, i.e. those with no opercular plates, and
(c) the number of dog whelks in the same quadrat.

Repeat the procedure ten times and use an average of the results.

Questions

(1) Is there any relationship between the number of empty barnacle cases and the number of dog whelks in the same area?
(2) When explaining the relationship, what basic assumption are you making which may invalidate your conclusion?
(3) Why are the dog whelks under-estimated?

Winkles

Exercise 12: to investigate how winkles maintain their position on the shore

Background

See pages 16–17 on zonation.

Materials

Nail varnish or ICI Belco 300 paint (can be painted on wet surfaces); tape measure; key (see p. 4).

Time

1 week.

Method

N.B. Beware of confusing young rough winkles with nerite winkles or young edible winkles with rough winkles (see key on p. 4).

Collect at least 50 specimens of all available species of *Littorina*. Mark them with nail varnish or Belco 300 paint. Place them all together in a region which can be located 24 h later. Measure the distance travelled and the direction for all the individuals at 24-h intervals for one week. Record the numbers which have returned to their normal zones. The Chi-squared test can be applied to the numbers if they exceed 50 to test the null hypothesis (see p. 39).

The same procedure may be carried out with species of top shells.

Question

Suggest an explanation for the homing behaviour of winkles and devise experiments to support your hypotheses.

Exercise 13: to investigate adaptive colouration in the flat winkle, *Littorina littoralis*

N.B. This exercise should be strictly limited to a small number of students because areas of algae have to be removed to be weighed and destruction of the habitat must be avoided. All animals must be handled with care and returned to the shore after use. The investigation could be carried out in conjunction with one on biomass (see p. 27).

Materials

½ m² quadrat; trowel; spring balance.

Time

30 min on the shore; 1 h in the laboratory.

Method

Select an area with a dense covering of wrack. Remove and weigh all the algae in an area ½ m². Count all the flat winkles in the same area.

N.B. some are very small and very well camouflaged. Sort out the winkles into various colour varieties. Repeat the exercise and find an average for numbers per m². Repeat the exercise for various species of wracks.

Questions

(1) Explain any relationship between

    (a) numbers of winkles and weight of algae,
    (b) colour of shell and the species of algae,
    (c) numbers of winkles and species of algae.

(2) Does the flat winkle eat adult wracks? Suggest a simple laboratory investigation to support your hypothesis.

(3) Do birds walk on the algae to feed? Use this observation to determine whether there is any selective pressure on certain colour varieties.

Algae

Exercise 14: a comparison of the age distribution of populations of bladder wrack and knotted wrack

Background

In the bladder wrack, pairs of bladders form each April. In knotted wrack, one bladder per branch per year is developed (see Fig. 25). In both species, parts may be lost after storms or after reproduction. The ecological significance of this exercise is to be able to assess the success of each or either species in varying conditions of wave exposure.

Figure 25 *Ascophyllum nodosum* with the epiphytic *Polysiphonia* sp. (photo courtesy of D. E. Rees).

Materials	*Time*
Quadrat.	1 h.

Method

Select 1 m² of a sheltered shore covered with a mixture of knotted wrack and bladder wrack as co-dominants. Count the number of complete plants growing in the 1 m². Repeat this for an exposed shore. (Use the biologically defined exposure scale, p. 23, to judge the degree of exposure.)

Questions

(1) Is there any relationship between:

   (a) the degree of exposure and number of plants?
   (b) the number of bladders per branch and the age of the plant?
   (c) the total number of bladders produced on a plant of known age and the degree of exposure to wave action?
   (d) the length of the plant and the degree of branching?

(2) In the case of knotted wrack, is there any relationship between the age of the plant and the amount of *Polysiphonia* sp. present? If you can suggest a relationship, explain it.

(3) Is the branching of bladder wrack dichotomous as most text books say it is? If not, suggest an explanation.

(4) Formulate a pattern of branching which will enable you to predict the probable sequence of subsequent branching in all the species of wracks present.

Sand and mud

Background

Few people become aware of the abundance of life in sand or mud unless they are prepared to dig for it. Little evidence of life below the sand appears on its surface but even the most casual observer must see the casts of the egested material of the lugworm. The more inquisitive will notice holes or depressions in the sand of up to 20 mm in diameter, near the strand line. These, and the ubiquitous empty shells, are the clues to the ecosystem within the sand. The evolutionary selective pressures of such an unstable environment have produced an extremely eccentric assortment of animals. The perfection of the burrowing habit has led to their survival. A firm substrate for attachment is absent, and in order to remain on the shore, animals must either burrow or be small enough to live among particles as interstitial fauna.

Interstitial spaces give sand its property of capillarity and causes water retention at low tide. Desiccation is a problem only on the highest level of the beach, where a specialised fauna, almost fully terrestrial by nature, relies on the dead and decaying remains in the strand line for food and shelter. Within the burrows of the middle and lower shore, physical conditions are very stable. Even on the hottest days of summer, when the surface sand dries, the temperature 200 mm below the surface is almost the same as that of the sea. Where estuaries occur, or where rain water percolates from cliffs, streams of fresh water pass over the sand at low tide. Surprisingly, the chloride concentration 300 mm below the surface is the same as that of sea water. The fauna of such regions burrow to avoid salinity changes.

All sandy beaches, apart from those receiving the most extreme wave action, will contain some fauna. The most exposed sand has little organic matter to attract animals and, because a source of food is a prerequisite for any form of heterotrophic life, it is not surprising that paucity of fauna is a characteristic of sandy shores subjected to prevailing winds and wave action.

Zonation occurs on sandy shores but it is not so dependent on the degree of exposure to desiccation as the zonation of rocky shores. Also, the seaward slope of the beach is not usually as well marked on sand as it is on rock.

How can one distinguish a sandy shore from a muddy shore? This is a difficult question, answered subjectively by identifying its inhabitants, or objectively with the use of a pedologist's scale for particle size, i.e.

Particle size	Diameter of particle (mm)
coarse sand	2.0–0.2
fine sand	0.2–0.02
silt	0.02–0.002
clay	less than 0.002

Muddy shores are subjected to little or no wave action. The sheltered conditions allow silt to be deposited and become mixed with the sand. In estuarine regions, the seaward end of the shore contains a greater proportion of sand than mud but at the river mouth the mud is pure and viscous. Once a shovel or foot is placed in this, the odour of hydrogen sulphide becomes obvious and the area seems less than a desirable residence for any animal. The hydrogen sulphide is generated as a result of a complex bacterial process in the sulphur cycle. The level at which anaerobic bacteria exists varies from 0.5 m below the surface in sheltered conditions, to 10 m on more exposed shores. Bacteria reduce ferric oxide to ferric sulphide. The colour of the mud changes and can be seen in profile: brown at the top; then yellow – grey; then black. The black layer smells of hydrogen sulphide when exposed to air. Hardly any aerobic life exists below the black layer with the exception of the lugworm. The apparently inhospitable substrate of mud is made even more unattractive to animals when it occurs in estuaries because of the constant fluctuation of salinity. Only the best adapted homoiosmotic species can survive such conditions.

Exercise 15: to investigate a zonation pattern in sand or mud

Exercise 16: to investigate any relationships between species present and (a) particle size, (b) organic matter and (c) diatoms

Materials

Tape measure (60 m) or a rope marked at 1 m intervals; quadrat; shovel; sieve; container for carrying water; containers for collecting substrate samples. Key (see pp. 8–15).

Time

3 h per exercise.

Method

Starting at the strand line on sand or at the last terrestrial plant on estuarine mud, lay out a tape towards the sea. Place a quadrat on the first station and count all the living animals on the surface of ½ m². Dig ½ m² to a depth of 0.5 m. Collect all the animals by washing through a sieve. Count and record the buried animals. Take a small sample of substrate and label it for analysis in the laboratory. Repeat the procedure at convenient intervals (depending on the length of shore) along the tape so that you reach the sea at the time of low tide.

In the laboratory

Materials

A microscope with high power magnification; microscope slides and cover slips; a stage graticule or a haemocytometer; bunsen, tripod, crucible; balance.

Time

3 h in the laboratory.

Method

Determine the organic content of a small amount of each sample by weighing, burning, and re-weighing to constant weights. Examine a sample of substrate to determine the average number of diatoms per unit area of the haemocytometer. Determine the average particle size of the substrate in your samples.

Record all your data in the form of histograms (numbers of species against distance from station 0). Tabulate your data on diatoms, particle size, organic content and distance from station 0.

Discuss your observations.

Questions

(1) Work out a food web (see p. 73) for the shore using only the species you have recorded.
(2) Which are the main producers?
(3) Suggest why the carnivores are under-sampled.

Exercise 17: investigations on populations of lugworms

Materials

Shovels; tape measure; Chi-squared probability tables.

Time

At least 1 h.

Method

Mark out 5 m² on an area of dense lugworm casts (see Fig. 26). Without disturbing the area, count the number of casts. Roughly 100 mm away from each cast is a depression. Place your shovel parallel to the cast and depression and systematically dig the area. Count all the living lugworms. Return them to the area. Apply the Chi-squared test to the numbers (see p. 39).

Questions

Explain why the number of casts is liable to be an under-estimate of the number of worms. Why would this error be more obvious in an area where a stream runs over the shore?

Figure 26   Casts of lugworms at low tide indicating a dense population beneath the sand (photo courtesy of D. E. Rees).

Exercise 18: an investigation of interstitial fauna

Background

There is an ecosystem of the intertidal sandy shore invisible to the unaided eye. It includes unicellular algae and a variety of microfauna. The algae must be viewed at a magnification of at least 100 times to be seen clearly, but may be so numerous that they form a yellowish-brown film on the surface of the sand. Some often have symmetrical, aesthetically pleasing, geometrical shapes. Others have flagella with which they swim in the film of water between the sand grains. The microscopic world of the interstices between the sand grains is really very extensive. Although the grains are touching one another, there are many spaces between their irregular shapes. The capillarity of the spaces is responsible for water retention, and in this water organisms can live. A bucket of sand is only 80 per cent sand, the rest is space.

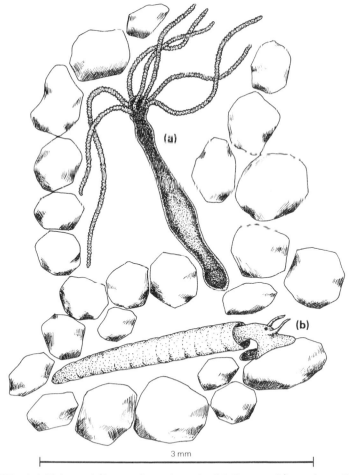

Figure 27   (a) *Halammohydra* sp. (a cnidarian); (b) *Caecum glabrum* (a mollusc).

When filled with water, this space forms a potential ecosystem. Within the sand the organisms are protected from changes in salinity and temperature. Interstitial species are found in the substrate of beds of freshwater lakes, water-logged soil, and in the littoral and sublittoral zones of the marine environment. A distinction between the interstitial fauna of the latter two areas is difficult to make. The structure of the substrate influences the type of microfauna present. A predominantly siliceous deposit supports a fauna which is different to that of a mixture of shell and sand, and both possess a fauna which differs from that of mud. Most major phyla have representatives living among sand grains. In order to be classed as truly interstitial fauna, they must move between the sand grains without displacing them.

Characteristics of interstitial fauna
Apart from Protozoa, which have larger representatives in sand than in most other environments, other phyla have evolved miniature interstitial types (see Figs 27 and 28). The optimum size for interstitial life is a length of

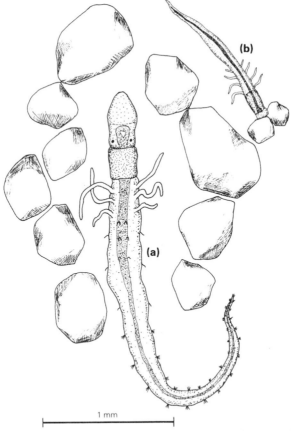

1 mm

Figure 28　(a) *Psammodrilus balanoglossoides* (an annelid); (b) *Psammodriloides fauveli* (an annelid).

0.5 mm to 3 mm (Swedmark 1964). Most phyla have these miniature forms. There is even a miniature sea-cucumber found in some sublittoral sand. Animals from the interstices of mud are even smaller – they rarely reach a length of 1.0 mm. Adaptation, resulting in simplification of organ systems, is obvious in many types and possibly the result of neoteny.

Interstitial animals usually have a worm-like shape or are flattened dorso-ventrally. A toughened body wall, which protects them from being crushed by the sand grains, is a feature of many forms. The body wall may be reinforced by spicules, e.g. in ciliates and molluscs. The ability to contract also helps some types avoid mechanical injury, and is seen in some ciliates, flat worms and molluscs. In a constantly moving environment, adhesive organs are useful to maintain the animal's position. Such organs take the form of glands, or in the case of some arthropods, hooks. The absence of light and the reduction of most exteroreceptors has emphasised the need for statocysts to aid orientation.

Considerable evolutionary convergence in structure between phyla with interstitial representatives has occurred – widely separated groups look alike. Convergence of behaviour has also taken place. Many groups use ciliary locomotion, e.g. ciliates, flat worms, annelids and molluscs. Writhing movements take place in crustaceans. Swedmark (1964) separates the interstitial fauna into four ecological categories on the basis of their methods of obtaining food:

(a) predators, e.g. cnidarians (coelenterates) and flat worms;
(b) diatom and epigrowth feeders, e.g. nematodes, crustaceans, rotifers and some annelids;
(c) detritus feeders, e.g. nematodes and some annelids;
(d) suspension feeders, e.g. one rare species of sea-mat.

Reproductive methods and behaviour ensure a high degree of parental care which is unusual for most invertebrates. Few eggs are produced and a pelagic larval phase is rare. Some are ovo-viviparous, others have brood pouches for incubation, and a few produce cocoons or single adhesive eggs. The mobility of the sand makes egg laying hazardous as it is unlikely that the eggs would remain in the surface layers without some protection or modification.

Materials

Measuring cylinder (1 l); sieve (mesh not less than 220 per cm²); 7 per cent magnesium chloride; pipette; microscope; slides and cover slips.

Time

1 h.

Method

Scoop out small quantities of sand into the cylinder until you have 100 cm³. Fill the cylinder with carefully filtered sea water, i.e. filtered through the sieve. In order to make clinging forms relax add a 7 per cent solution of narcotic, magnesium chloride (5 cm³). Shake the mixture and pour the liquid through the sieve as before. The stranded animals can then be carefully removed from the mesh with a fine pipette and must be examined under a microscope as soon as possible. If their examination is not possible immediately, preserve the catch in 4 per cent formalin.

Questions

(1) How many representatives of different phyla have you collected?
(2) List the adaptations to the environment shown by the animals collected.

Filter feeding

Exercise 1: an investigation of the filter feeding method of a sponge

Background

It was a short evolutionary step from a cell capable of moving through water using a flagellum to an aggregation of cells setting up a current by means of co-ordinated lashing. The end product is a sponge which may have evolved either by failure of flagellated cells to separate after division, or by similar cells aggregating to form a colonial animal. Sponges constitute the phylum Porifera a name that describes their porous nature. The pores lead to flagellated cavities lined by collared cells. These resemble certain flagellate protozoans but have lost their ancestral individuality. The lashing of the flagella forces the water through the sponge and out through a larger opening, the osculum. (See Figs 29, 30a & b.) Suspended particles are trapped by the flagella and some are ingested by the collared cells (see Figs 30c & d). The food includes plankton and some species have been shown to feed on bacteria.

Materials

Carmine powder; pipette; binocular microscope.

Time

30 min.

Method

The crumb of bread sponge, *Halichondria panicea* and the purse sponge, *Grantia compressa* are usually the most readily available British sponges, widely distributed on the lower shore.

Place a healthy, freshly collected sponge, with a distinct osculum, in a shallow dish of sea water. Observe the animal with a binocular microscope.

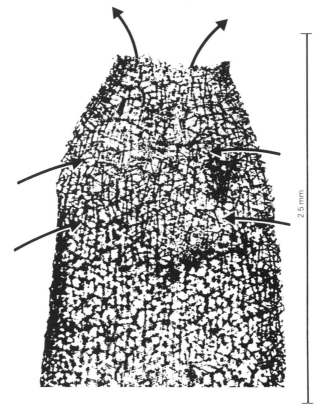

Figure 29 Part of the branching sponge, *Leucoselenia botryoides*, highly magnified to show the skeletal spicules. The arrows indicate the direction of water movement.

2.5 mm

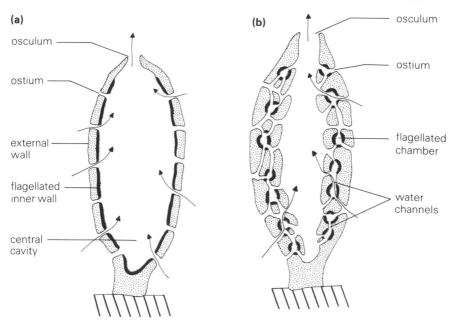

(a)

osculum

ostium

external wall

flagellated inner wall

central cavity

(b)

osculum

ostium

flagellated chamber

water channels

(c)

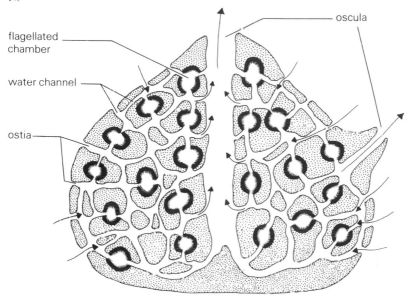

flagellated chamber

water channel

ostia

oscula

(d)

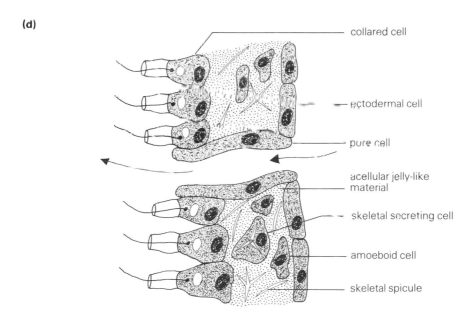

collared cell

ectodermal cell

pore cell

acellular jelly-like material

skeletal secreting cell

amoeboid cell

skeletal spicule

Figure 30 (a) Section through a simple sponge (arrows indicate direction of water movement); (b) section through a more complex sponge; (c) section through a complex sponge; (d) an enlarged longitudinal section through the wall of a sponge.

Take some carmine particles suspended in sea water, in a fine pipette. Observe the end of the pipette while placing it into the osculum. Release the particles. Remove the pipette. Observe the clouds of particles as they exude from the osculum.

Questions

(1) Is there an even flow outwards?
(2) Is the flow in the form of pulsations?
(3) Is the rate of flow the same at the time of low tide as it is at the time of high tide?

Place some more particles on the surface of the sponge. Describe the movement of the particles.

Ciliary feeding in mussels

Background

A distinction between flagella and cilia is possible by reference to size and movement. Flagella move by means of waves which travel along them, and are longer than cilia which lash stiffly through the water like oars. Cilia are present in almost every phylum except the arthropods. The result of ciliary action is the same as that of flagellar movement, i.e. the capture of suspended particles. Most ciliary feeders are marine and often produce copious mucus in which particles are trapped and transported to the mouth. Selection of the type of food is rare but particle size is recognised by many types. As with flagella, the feeding role of cilia has developed as a secondary trend in an originally locomotory organelle. Most ciliate protozoans exhibit ciliary locomotion whereas more complex metazoans use cilia to pass materials over or through their bodies.

Bivalve molluscs are filter feeders par excellence. Their ctenidia ('gills') have reached gigantic proportions in most littoral types and perform functions of gaseous exchange, collection and sorting of suspended material (see Figs 31a, b, c, d and 32a & b). On either side of the foot of a mussel, each net-like ctenidium consists of a central axis with rows of ciliated filaments. Using the high power magnification of a microscope, groups of cilia can be seen in a definite pattern in transverse sections of the filaments. Near the mouth are special cilia which reject particles too large for ingestion.

Littoral filter feeders collect an enormous amount of plankton. Parasites and commensals take advantage of this potential food supply. Ciliate protozoans, crustaceans and a nemertine often live between the valves of mussels or around the pharynx of sea squirts. The pea crab (see Fig. 33) is perhaps the most spectacular commensal of mussels. It can be found in other bivalves and sea squirts and shows adaptations characteristic of parasites, e.g. reduced appendages and exteroreceptors.

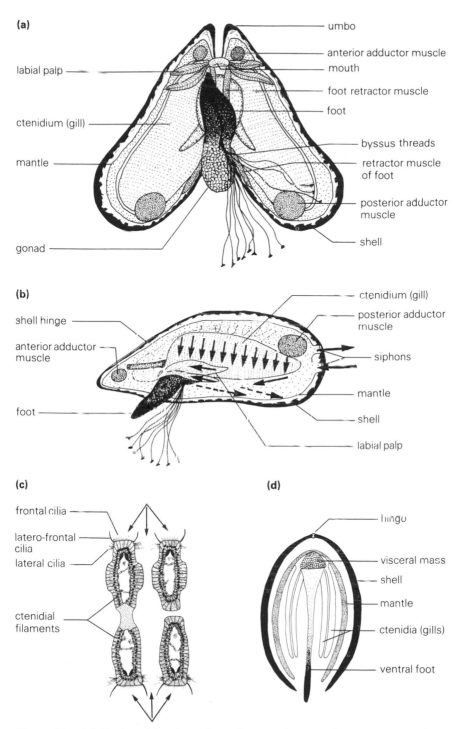

Figure 31 (a) *Mytilus edulis*, drawn from the ventral aspect after opening its valves; (b) diagrammatic lateral view of a mussel to show the feeding and respiratory currents (solid arrows indicate direction of water flow; broken arrows indicate the path taken by egested materials); (c) diagrammatic transverse section through the ctenidial ('gill') filaments of a bivalve when viewed through a microscope; (d) diagrammatic cross section through a bivalve.

(a)

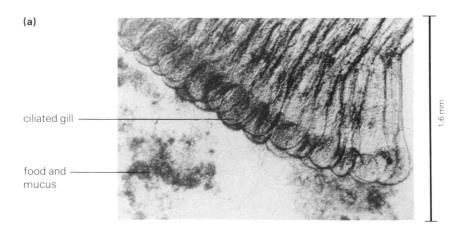

ciliated gill

food and mucus

1.6 mm

(b)

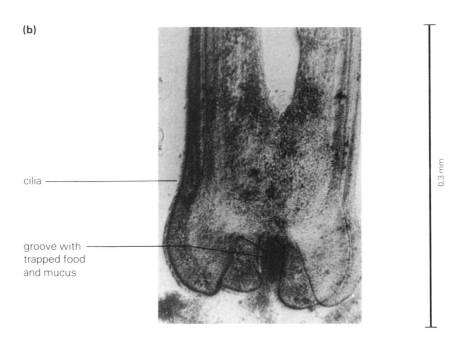

cilia

groove with trapped food and mucus

0.3 mm

Figure 32 (a) Photomicrograph of the ctenidia ('gills') of a mussel trapping particles. x 250. (b) Photomicrograph showing the ctenidial cilia. x 600.

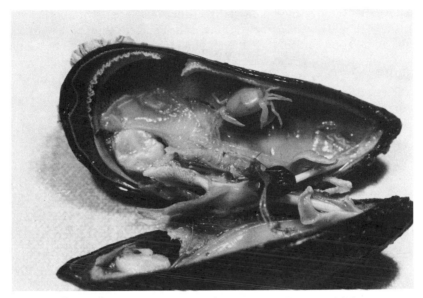

Figure 33   The commensal pea crab, *Pinnotheres pisum*, inside a mussel (photo courtesy of D. E. Rees).

Exercise 2: an investigation of the feeding method of the common mussel

Materials

Carmine powder; pipette; pen knife (*not* a scalpel with a detachable blade); binocular microscope.

Time

1 h 30 min.

Method

Use the edible mussel, *Mytilus edulis*. Place a healthy specimen in well aerated sea water. Leave it for 15 min and then observe that the shells are partly open. Identify the siphons (see Fig. 31b) and pipette some carmine particles near them. Draw a side view showing the inhalent and exhalent streams.

Take the mussel in your hand and insert a pen knife between the shells. (Do not use a scalpel with a detachable blade as it often snaps and could cause a serious wound.) Twist the blade clockwise. The valves should now open wider. Remove the blade and pull the shells apart with your fingers. The shells should now be attached only at the ligament (hinge). Use one side of the animal only and identify the gills and labial palps at the mouth. Place the half in a dish of sea water and draw it. Pipette some carmine particles near the remains of the inhalent siphon. Observe the movement of the particles with a binocular microscope. Record the movement of the particles by drawing a plan and indicate with arrows the path taken.

Suggest how the particles are carried along.

Setous feeding in barnacles

Background

Barnacles are the most abundant animals on British rocky shores and act like an infinite number of grasping hands when they are covered by the sea. They are crustaceans which lie with their heads downwards and draw particles towards their mouths with antennae and setous legs (see Fig. 34). The setae are minute hair-like structures which cover the appendages of most arthropods. While using them for filtering, barnacles remain protected within miniature calcareous volcanoes which can be closed by opercular plates. Plankton is retained by the setae and passed to the mouth. The locomotory appendages of barnacles have taken on a food gathering function and are called cirri. Only the larvae use appendages for locomotion; the adults are

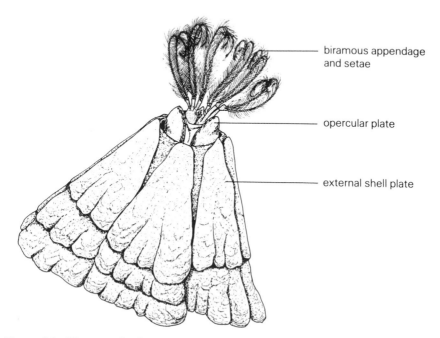

biramous appendage and setae

opercular plate

external shell plate

Figure 34 Diagram of a feeding barnacle.

completely sedentary. Once collected particles reach the head, they are wiped off the cirri by appendages surrounding the mouth. These also sort out edible from inedible particles. Organisms up to 1 mm long can be caught on the setae of the largest British species. The food comprises mainly planktonic larvae but phytoplankton, no more than 0.002 mm long, are also trapped. Bacteria can be wafted towards the mouth by the current set up by the beating cirri. They are then caught in a net formed by pairs of stationary cirri in the mouth. These cirri have an extremely fine net of setae with meshes only 1 μm across.

Exercise 3: an investigation of the feeding method of barnacles

Materials

Carmine powder; pipette; needle; binocular microscope; aeration pump.

Time

24 h.

Method

Place some freshly collected mussels with epizoic barnacles in a shallow dish with sea water. Observe them with a binocular microsope. Introduce some carmine powder with a pipette. Observations should take place over a period of 24 h, so aeration of the water will be necessary. Observe the opening of the opercular plates. Touch the open ones with a needle and observe how they close. Observe how the carmine particles are trapped

Questions

(1) Are all the barnacles feeding at the same time?
(2) Are more feeding at the time corresponding to high tide than to low tide?

Observe the distribution pattern of adult barnacles on the mussel shell. Draw a plan diagram of the mussel shell to show the position of the siphons and the position of the barnacles. Explain any relationship. Is there more than one species of barnacle on the shell? (See Fig. 20a, b, c for identification.)

Sea-anemones

Background

The radial symmetry of the armed tentacles of the Cnidaria is an adaptation for trapping swimming animals (see Fig. 35). Littoral types use cells which are modified with stinging threads (see Figs 36a and b). These can inject paralysing chemicals into their prey. The prey consists of small inverte-brates, such as crustaceans, which are pushed into the single opening of the enteron for digestion. The sea-anemones and sea-firs (Hydrozoa) feed by paralysing and holding the prey on the tentacles. Adjacent ones bend over to continue the stinging and holding until all begin to move to the mouth. Indigestible remains are later voided through the same opening. Each stinging cell is a double-walled capsule filled with a paralysing chemical, set in the outer surface of the tentacles. Each contains a coiled hollow thread, sometimes barbed at the base. At the outer end of the capsule is a sensory trigger. When this is touched, the thread is shot out. It turns inside out as it is

Figure 35   Tentacles of the jewel anemone, *Corynactis viridis*.

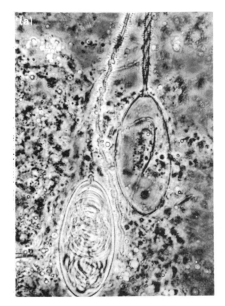

Figure 36 (a) Stinging cells of *Corynactis viridis*. (The stinging thread can be seen coiled within the capsule.) x 450. (b) A discharged stinging thread of *Corynactis viridis*. (Note the barbs towards the base of the thread.) x 450.

ejected, its fine point pierces the skin of the prey and the fluid flows through the hollow thread. Some types of stinging cells stick to the prey and a third type wraps itself around the victim.

Few animals eat sea-anemones because of their defence mechanism but some predators are able to turn this to their own advantage in a most unusual way. Certain sea-slugs (Nudibranchiata) eat sea-anemones and use their stinging cells for their own defence (see Fig. 37). The stinging cells are taken to the mollusc's digestive system and migrate to the epithelium of the predator. If the sea-slug is touched, it discharges the stinging cells as if it were a cnidarian.

Exercise 4: an investigation of responses of sea-anemones

Materials

Monocular microscope; microscope slides and cover slips; methylene blue; glass rod; dilute acid and dilute alkali.

Time

1 h.

Figure 37 The grey sea-slug, *Aeolidia papillosa*, crawling over a stone encrusted by the keeled tube worm, *Pomatoceros triqueter* (photo courtesy of D. E. Rees).

Method

Use the beadlet anemone, *Actinia equina*. Observe the response of the tentacles while it is under water. Stimulate the tentacles mechanically with a glass rod and then stimulate them with a glass rod dipped in the extract from a mussel.

Observe the effect of the following on a single tentacle: (a) washed sand grains; (b) food particles.

Examine a discharged stinging cell under the microscope as follows. Moisten a cover slip with saliva and allow it to dry. Touch a tentacle with the cover slip. Lightly stain the cover slip with methylene blue and examine it under high power.

Cut off a tentacle, mount it on a slide and cover it with a cover slip. Observe the response of the stinging cells to mechanical stimulation with a glass rod and to a glass rod dipped in the extract from a mussel. Explain any differences. Observe the responses of the stinging cells when the tentacles are mounted in (a) sea water, (b) dilute acid and (c) dilute alkali.

Food webs

Quantitative illustrations of feeding patterns are not always so easy to construct because communities are not always so densely packed as those of rocky shores and mussel beds. Theoretical models of food chains and webs can always be made with a knowledge of the feeding habits of members of an ecosystem. Figure 38 shows a possible food web that can be applied to any environment. Figure 39 shows a theoretical food web for a rocky shore.

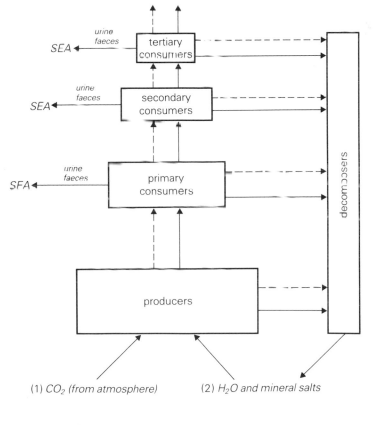

(1) CO_2 (from atmosphere)   (2) H_2O and mineral salts

Key

———▶ inorganic nutrients

----▶ organic foods

Figure 38 Nutrient flow.

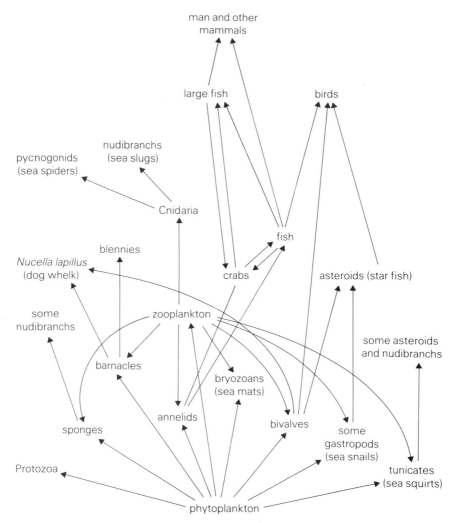

Figure 39 A theoretical food web of a rocky shore using phytoplankton as the primary producer.

As a result of your observations of the variety of life on the shores that you have studied, construct a theoretical food web beginning with attached seaweed. Use the information on feeding given below.

A summary of the food and feeding methods of common littoral invertebrates

Animal or group	Type of feeder	Food
sponges	flagellate	plankton
Cnidaria	carnivorous with stinging cells	animals small enough to be caught
Nemertea (ribbon worms)	carnivorous with proboscis	annelids and crustaceans
Annelida (true worms)		
tube worms	ciliary	plankton and detritus
rag worms	scavengers	invertebrates and carrion
scale worms	detritous	detritus
Arthropoda		
Crustacea		
slaters (Isopoda, e.g. sea-slater)	scavengers	algal detritus
sand-hoppers	mainly scavengers, some carnivores	algal detritus and invertebrates
barnacles	setous filters	plankton
porcelain 'crabs'	setous filters	detritus
true crabs	scavengers	most plants and animals
Pycnogonida		
sea-spiders	fluid feeders with piercing mouth parts	Cnidaria and sea-mats
Mollusca		
chitons (coat of mail shells)	herbivorous with radula	algal sporelings
bivalves	ciliary	plankton
limpets		algal sporelings
blue rayed limpet		kelp
top shells	herbivorous with radula	algal detritus and fine red algae
winkles		diatoms, detritus and algal sporelings
cowries		sea-squirts
dog whelks		barnacles, mussels, tube worms, snails
common whelk	carnivorous with radula	carrion, crabs, annelids, bivalves
sea-slugs		sponges, sea-squirts, Cnidaria, sea-mats
Ectoprocta (sea-mats)	ciliary	plankton
Echinodermata		
brittle stars		
surface dwelling	carnivores	annelids and crustaceans
burrowing	ciliary	suspended matter
sea-cucumbers	tentacular with mucus	detritus
starfish	use of tube feet and extrusion of stomach	molluscs and carrion
sea urchins	omnivorous	algae, carrion, barnacles

Tube worms

Exercise 5: an investigation of fertilisation in the keeled tube worm, *Pomatoceros triqueter*

Background
This animal has an elongated, triangular, calcareous tube, about 50 mm long. It lives on the middle and lower shore, cemented to rocks or shells, and is widely distributed. Like other tube worms, it is a filter feeder. It can be used to demonstrate fertilisation and egg cleavage.

Materials
Forceps; glass dish; blunt seeker; binocular and monocular microscopes; microscope slides and cover slips; pipette.

Time
30 min.

Method
Collect a suitable sized stone from the lower shore which has *Pomatoceros* sp. cemented to it. With coarse forceps, while the animals are under sea water in a dish, chip away the calcareous tube. Sometimes the worms can be forced out with a blunt seeker. Select a male (yellow body) and a female (red or violet body). Put one of each in a dish under a binocular microscope; cover them with sea water and observe.

The eggs and spermatozoa should be seen being released as soon as the animals have been removed from their tubes. Pipette some eggs and spermatazoa on to a microscope slide in sea water. Cover with a cover slip and observe under high power magnification.

Note how the spermatozoa swim around the eggs. Watch how the egg membrane swells. This is a sign that fertilisation has taken place.

Make drawings of the eggs

(a) when the membrane swells,
(b) 10 min later,
(c) 30 min later.

Note any difference in appearance of the egg after fertilisation.

Crabs

Exercise 6: an investigation of salinity tolerance of the shore crab, *Carcinus maenas*

Background

Homoiosmotic species are common in estuaries. They have the problem of adjusting their internal ion concentration when the ion concentration of their environment changes. If they were not successful at doing this, they would either gain or lose weight by osmosis as their environment became more or less salty. The common shore crab, *Carcinus maenas*, is such an animal. It has an almost ubiquitous distribution around Britain from the middle to the lower shore but is also found in estuaries and up to a mile from the sea. In order to be successful within this wide range of salinity, it has to have a very efficient regulatory mechanism for pumping out excess water in an estuary and concentrating salts when in full strength sea water. There is a limit to the dilution that it can tolerate. This can be demonstrated as described below.

Materials

Ten, 250 cm³ beakers; syringes and needles; diluted sea water from 0.1 full strength to full strength – each beaker will contain 200 cm³ of sea water of a particular strength (see below); an accurate balance; aerator.

Time

1 h 30 min.

Method

Take ten specimens of common shore crab, of approximately the same size so that similar surface areas are exposed to the environment. Make a series of progressively more dilute sea water, ranging from full strength to 0.1 full strength. Take a hypodermic syringe and draw off the water from the gill chambers (see Fig. 40). (The crabs can store water in the gill chambers and

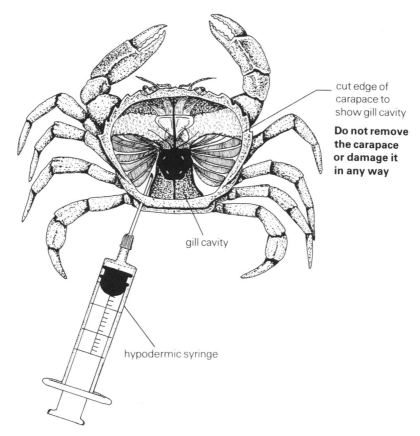

cut edge of
carapace to
show gill cavity

**Do not remove
the carapace
or damage it
in any way**

gill cavity

hypodermic syringe

Figure 40 Diagrammatic representation of the method used to draw off water from the gill chamber of a crab.

this would cause the initial weights to vary.) Weigh each crab and record its weight. Label each crab in order to be able to identify it later. Place each crab in a beaker containing 200 cm³ of sea water, i.e. crab A in full strength, crab B in 0.9, crab C in 0.8 sea water etc. Aerate each beaker and leave it for 1 h. Take each crab, remove water from the gill chamber as before, and re-weigh. Use the average results of all the students carrying out the exercise. Other species of crabs could be used as a comparison.

Questions

(1) What is the maximum dilution that this species can tolerate?
(2) Discuss the limitations of the method used.

Algae

Exercise 7: the separation of pigments of algae

Background

Botanists classify algae according to their colours (see key on p. 6). Red and brown types have chlorophyll but its colour is masked by the presence of other pigments. At least two views are held concerning the importance of the red (phycoerythrin) and brown (fucoxanthin) pigments. When submerged, algae receive light which has been filtered through various depths of sea water. Consequently they are deprived of most red and yellow light, which is absorbed by chlorophyll. The red and brown pigments may be able to absorb the blue and green light and so obtain energy for photosynthesis. The other view is that the pigments protect the chlorophyll against too much light and that seaweeds are shade plants with particularly sensitive chlorophyll. The pigments can be separated by paper chromatography.

Materials

Algae, ethanol, acetone or petroleum ether; chromatography paper and tanks; pestle and mortar; measuring cylinders.

Time

1 h.

Method

N.B. The pigments are labile and easily decomposed. All work should be carried out in diffused light. Chromatograms should be spotted rapidly and placed immediately into the tank. The run should take place in the dark and preferably in a refrigerator. Extracting solvents should be pre-cooled. Care must be taken with the toxic inflammable solvents.

(1) Pour 50 cm³ of the solvent (acetone : petroleum ether (40–60°C) 30 : 70 by volume) into the tank. Replace the lid. Allow 15 min for

some solvent to evaporate and saturate the air space in the tank. In the remainder of the extraction, remove the lid *as little as possible*, as the solvents are very volatile.

(2) Take 1 g of fresh alga. Cut it into small pieces and add a little sand and grind it with a pestle and mortar for 20 s. Place the ground-up material in a 50 cm³ stoppered tube, add 40 cm³ of acetone, stopper and shake vigorously for 10 s. Allow it to stand for 10 min. Add 4 cm³ water and shake the mixture.

(3) Add 3 cm³ petroleum ether and shake the mixture vigorously for 10 s. Allow the mixture to stand until the solvents separate. The pigments will almost all be confined to the petroleum ether (upper layer). The plant will be white.

(4) Remove the upper layer with a pipette.

(5) Prepare the chromatography paper.

(6) Spot the solution on to the origin, using minute drops and keeping the origin diameter less than 5 mm. Apply four separate drops so that the colour of the extract remains after solvent evaporation.

(7) Place the paper in the tank and close the lid. Allow the chromatogram to run for 30 min in the dark and preferably in a refrigerator.

(8) Remove the chromatogram and allow it to dry in the dark for 2 min. Note the pigments.

The red alga, *Laurencia pinnatifida* and laver, *Porphyra umbilicalis* often appear brown or black but they can be proved to be red by the above method.

Exercise 8: to investigate desiccation in algae

Background

The amount of desiccation that littoral organisms can tolerate is related to the zone in which they normally live (see p. 16). This can be demonstrated with seaweeds.

Materials

Flat trays; electric fan or similar; balance.

Time

At least 12 h.

Method

Take equal fresh weights of samples of different species of wracks, collected at the same time. Use whole plants as far as possible. Spread each species on flat trays of known area, one species per tray. Expose an equal surface area to desiccation on each tray. Record the percentage loss of weight for each species each hour. Plot the percentage loss of weight against time for each species. Relate your results to zonation (see p. 16).

Exercise 9: to investigate the effectiveness of algal pigments in photosynthesis

Background

The intensity and wavelength of light are limiting factors in photosynthesis. Algae which live in deeper water receive low light intensity and mostly green–blue light, whereas algae on the upper shore are exposed to much more light of the complete spectrum.

Aim

To investigate the value of the red pigment in sublittoral Rhodophyceae.

Time

2 h.

Materials

Four stoppered 500 cm³ flasks; sea water; green algae (use *Enteromorpha* sp. or *Ulva* sp.); red algae (use *Polysiphonia* sp. or *Chondrus* sp.); electric lamp; two green–blue photographic filters; two neutral density filters; oxygen meter.

Method

Fill four 500 cm³ flasks with sea water. Add equal amounts of green algae to two of the flasks, A and B, and similar amounts of red algae to the other two, C and D. Place the stoppers in the flasks. Put the green–blue filters in front of A and C and a neutral density filter in front of B and D. Use an oxygen meter to determine the relative concentration of oxygen in the water in each flask compared with fully oxygen saturated water. Expose the flasks to strong light for 2 h. Measure the oxygen concentration as before. Tabulate the results under the following headings: flask; initial oxygen; and final oxygen.

Questions

(1) What is the purpose of the neutral density filter?
(2) Discuss the value of the red pigment in red algae.

Exercise 10: to investigate the gas composition of the vesicles of *Ascophyllum nodosum*

Background

The obvious survival value of vesicles on algae is to aid floatation in the optimum position for photosynthesis. Analysis of the gas in the vesicles could suggest a function of carbon dioxide storage as an additional aid to efficient photosynthesis.

Aim

To determine the composition of the vesicles of *Ascophyllum nodosum*

Materials

Olive oil; J tube; alkaline pyrogallol; caustic soda; scalpel; *Ascophyllum* sp. with as large vesicles as possible.

Method

Cut open the bladder of *Ascophyllum* sp. (*Fucus vesiculosus* bladders are more difficult to use because of their smaller size) under oil. The contents can be collected over oil for analysis of carbon dioxide and oxygen concentration by the J tube method*.

Questions

(1) Is there any change in composition (a) after exposure of the algae to sun at low tide? (b) from the top and bottom of heaps of algae found in the strand line?
(2) Suggest why all algae do not have bladders.

---

* *Biological science laboratory book. A technical guide*, P. Fry (ed.), 119–20. Nuffield Advanced Science. Published for the Nuffield Foundation by Penguin Books, 1971.

Bibliography

General accounts of the sea shore biology

Amos, W. H. 1969. *The life of the seashore*. New York: McGraw-Hill.
Barrett, J. H. 1975. *Life on the sea shore*. London: Collins.
Evans, S. M. and J. M. Hardy 1970. *Seashore and sand dunes*. London: Heinemann.
Newell, R. C. 1970. *The biology of intertidal animals*. London: Lagos Press.
Nicol, J. A. C. 1960. *The biology of marine animals*. London: Pitman.
Southward, A. J. 1965. *Life on the sea shore*. London: Heinemann.
Yonge, C. M. 1949. *The seashore*. Glasgow: Collins.

Rocky shore ecology

Ballantine, W. J. 1961. A biologically defined exposure scale for the comparative description of rocky shores. *Field Studies* **1** (3), 1–19.
Lewis, R. J. 1964. *The ecology of rocky shores*. London: English University Press.
Miles, P. H. and H. B. Miles 1966. *Seashore ecology*. London: Hulton.
Tait, R. V. 1972. *Elements of marine ecology*. London: Butterworth.

Sand and mud

Barnes, R. S. K. 1974. *Estuarine biology*. London: Edward Arnold.
Brafield, A. E. 1978. *Life in sandy shores*. London: Edward Arnold.
Eltringham, S. K. 1971. *Life in mud and sand*. London: English University Press.
Green, J. 1968. *The biology of estuarine animals*. London: Sidgwick & Jackson.
Swedmark, B. 1964. The interstitial fauna of marine sand. *Biol Rev*. **39**, 1–42.

Monographs and identification guides

General
Barrett, J. H. and C. M. Yonge 1977. *Pocket guide to the sea shore*. Glasgow: Collins.
Campbell, A. C. and J. Nicholls 1976. *The Hamlyn guide to the seashore and shallow seas of Britain and Europe*. London: Hamlyn.
Eales, N. B. 1967. *The littoral fauna of the British Isles*. Cambridge: Cambridge University Press.
Newell, G. E. and R. C. Newell 1973. *Marine plankton*. London: Hutchinson.

Algae and Lichens
Boney, A. D. 1969. *A biology of marine algae*. London: Hutchinson.
Dickenson, C. I. 1963. *British seaweeds*. London: Spottiswood.

Eifion Jones, W. 1962. A key to the genera of the British marine algae. *Field Studies* **1** (4), 1–32.

Ferry, B. W. and J. W. Sheard 1969. Zonation of supra-littoral lichens on rocky shores around the Dale peninsula. (With a key for identification.) *Field Studies* **3** (1), 41–67.

Hiscocks, S. 1979. *A field key to the British brown seaweeds. Field Studies* **5** (1), 1–44.

Newton, L. 1931. *A handbook of the British seaweeds.* London: British Museum.

Sponges

Burton, M. 1963. *Revision of classification of calcareous sponges.* London: British Museum.

Cnidaria

Hainsworth, M. D. 1974. *Biological studies through the microscope: 2. Coelenterates and their food.* London: Macmillan.

Hinks, T. 1868. *History of the British hydroid zoophytes.* London: Gurney & Jackson.

Stephenson, T. A. 1928. *The British sea anemones.* London: Ray Society.

Nemertea

Gibson, R. 1972. *Nemerteans.* London: Hutchinson.

Annelida

Dales, R. P. 1970. *Annelids.* London: Hutchinson.

Nelson-Smith, A. and J. M. Gee 1966. Serpulid tubeworms around Dale. *Field Studies* **2** (3), 331–7.

Arthropoda

CRUSTACEA

Bassindale, R. 1964. *British barnacles with keys and notes for identification of species.* Lin. Soc. Syn. Brit. Fauna, no. 14.

Crisp, D. J. and A. J. Southward 1963. *Catalogue of main marine fouling organisms: 1. Barnacles.* Paris: OECD.

Crothers, J. H. 1967. The biology of the shore crab. *Field Studies* **2** (4), 407–34.

Naylor, E. 1972. *British marine isopods.* London: Academic Press.

Schmitt, W. L. 1973. *Crustaceans.* London: David & Charles.

PYCNOGONIDS (*sea spiders*)

King, P. E. and G. B. Crapp 1971. Littoral pycnogonids of the British Isles. *Field Studies* **3** (3), 455–80.

Molluscs

Beedham, G. E. 1972. *Identification of the British Mollusca.* London: Hulton.

Fretter, V. and A. Graham 1962. *British prosobranch molluscs.* London: Ray Society.

Graham, A. 1971. *British Prosobranchs* London: Academic Press.

McMillan, N. 1968. *British shells.* London: Warne.

Morton, J. E. 1970. *Molluscs.* London: Hutchinson.

Moyse, J. (in preparation). The distribution of the colour varieties of *L. obtusata* (L.) and *L. mariae* Sacchi and Rastelli, in the Dale area.

Sacchi, C. F. and M. Rastelli 1967. *Littorina mariae* nov. sp.: les différences morphologiques et écologiques, entre 'nains' et 'normaux' chez l'espèce *L. obtusata* (L.) et leur signification adaptative et évolutive. *Atti. Soc. It. Sci. Nat. Milan* **105**, 351–70.

Tebble, N. 1966. *British bivalve molluscs.* London: British Museum.

Thompson, T. E. 1976. *Biology of opisthobranch molluscs.* London: Ray Society.

Thompson, T. E. 1976. *British opisthobranch molluscs.* London: Academic Press.

Yonge, C. M. and Thompson, T. E. *Living marine molluscs.* Glasgow: Collins.

Bryozoa

Ryland, J. S. 1962. Biology and identification of intertidal Polyzoa. *Field Studies* **1** (4), 33–51.

Ryland, J. S. 1970. *Bryozoans.* London: Hutchinson.

Ryland, J. S. and P. J. Hayward 1977. *British anascan bryozoans.* London: Academic Press.

Echinoderms

Clark, A. M. 1968. *Starfishes and their relations.* London: British Museum.

Mortenson, T. 1927. *Handbook of echinoderms of the British Isles.* Oxford: Oxford University Press.

Nichols, D. 1969. *Echinoderms.* London: Hutchinson.

Tunicates

Berrill, N. J. 1950. *The Tunicata.* London: Ray Society.

Millar, R. H. 1970. *British Ascidians.* London. Academic Press.

Fish

Bagenal, T. B. 1974. *Identification of British fishes.* London: Hulton.

Wheeler, A. 1969. *The fishes of the British Isles and north-west Europe.* London: Macmillan.

Appendix

t test for two independent samples

	POPULATION 1			POPULATION 2	
Observation (x)	Deviation of observation from mean $(x - \bar{x}_1)$	Square of deviation $(x - \bar{x}_1)^2$	Observation (x)	Deviation of observation from mean $(x - \bar{x}_2)$	Square of deviation $(x - \bar{x}_2)^2$

Population 1	Population 2
Sum of observations $\Sigma x_1 =$	Sum of observations $\Sigma x_2 =$
Sum of squares of deviation $\Sigma(x - \bar{x}_1)^2 =$	Sum of squares of deviation $\Sigma(x - \bar{x}_2)^2 =$
No. of observations $n_1 =$	No. of observations $n_2 =$
Sum of squares $(SS_1) = \Sigma(x - \bar{x}_1)^2 =$	Sum of squares $(SS_2) = \Sigma(x - \bar{x}_2)^2 =$
Variance $V_1 = \dfrac{SS}{n_1 - 1} =$	Variance $(V_2) = \dfrac{SS}{n_2 - 1} =$
Standard deviation $(SD_1) = \sqrt{V_1}$	Standard deviation $(SD_2) = \sqrt{V_2}$
Mean of population 1 $(\bar{x}_1) = \dfrac{\Sigma x_1}{n_1} =$	Mean of population 2 $(\bar{x}_2) = \dfrac{\Sigma x_2}{n_2} =$
Standard error of mean of population 1 $(SE\,\bar{x}_1) = \sqrt{\dfrac{V_1}{n_1}} =$	Standard error of mean of population 2 $(SE\,\bar{x}_2) = \sqrt{\dfrac{V_2}{n_2}} =$

Standard error of difference between means of populations 1 and 2 $SE(\bar{x}_1 - \bar{x}_2) = \sqrt{SE\bar{x}_1^2 + SE\bar{x}_2^2} =$

$$t = \frac{\text{Difference between means of populations 1 and 2}}{\text{Standard error of difference}} = \frac{\bar{x}_1 - \bar{x}_2}{SE(\bar{x}_1 - \bar{x}_2)} =$$

Degrees of freedom for $t = (n_1 - 1) + (n_2 - 1) =$

Probability =

N.B. When using this method to compare samples of molluscs from two different shores, if the calculated value of t is less than that in the table (p. 89), the two samples may be from a single population and there is no evidence to the contrary. Their means do not differ significantly.

Statistical tables

Distribution of χ^2.

Degrees of freedom						Probability P						
	0.99	0.98	0.95	0.90	0.80	0.50	0.20	0.10	0.05	0.02	0.01	0.001
1	0.000	0.001	0.004	0.016	0.064	0.455	1.64	2.71	3.84	5.41	6.64	10.83
2	0.020	0.040	0.103	0.211	0.446	1.386	3.22	4.61	5.99	7.82	9.21	13.82
3	0.115	0.185	0.352	0.584	1.005	2.366	4.64	6.25	7.82	9.84	11.35	16.27
4	0.297	0.429	0.711	1.064	1.649	3.357	5.99	7.78	9.49	11.67	13.28	18.47
5	0.554	0.752	1.145	1.610	2.343	4.351	7.29	9.24	11.07	13.39	15.09	20.52
6	0.872	1.134	1.635	2.204	3.070	5.35	8.56	10.65	12.59	15.03	16.81	22.46
7	1.239	1.564	2.167	2.833	3.822	6.35	9.80	12.02	14.07	16.62	18.48	24.32
8	1.646	2.032	2.733	3.490	4.594	7.34	11.03	13.36	15.51	18.17	20.09	26.13
9	2.088	2.532	3.325	4.168	5.380	8.34	12.24	14.68	16.92	19.68	21.67	27.88
10	2.558	3.059	3.940	4.865	6.179	9.34	13.44	15.99	18.31	21.16	23.21	29.59
11	3.05	3.61	4.58	5.58	6.99	10.34	14.63	17.28	19.68	22.62	24.73	31.26
12	3.57	4.18	5.23	6.30	7.81	11.34	15.81	18.55	21.03	24.05	26.22	32.91
13	4.11	4.77	5.89	7.04	8.63	12.34	16.99	19.81	22.36	25.47	27.69	34.53
14	4.66	5.37	6.57	7.79	9.47	13.34	18.15	21.06	23.69	26.87	29.14	36.12
15	5.23	5.99	7.26	8.55	10.31	14.34	19.31	22.31	25.00	28.26	30.58	37.70
16	5.81	6.61	7.96	9.31	11.15	15.34	20.47	23.54	26.30	29.63	32.00	39.25
17	6.41	7.26	8.67	10.09	12.00	16.34	21.62	24.77	27.59	31.00	33.41	40.79
18	7.02	7.91	9.39	10.87	12.86	17.34	22.76	25.99	28.87	32.35	34.81	42.31
19	7.63	8.57	10.12	11.65	13.72	18.34	23.90	27.20	30.14	33.69	36.19	43.82
20	8.26	9.24	10.85	12.44	14.58	19.34	25.04	28.41	31.41	35.02	37.57	45.32
21	8.90	9.92	11.59	13.24	15.45	20.34	26.17	29.62	32.67	36.34	38.93	46.80
22	9.54	10.60	12.34	14.04	16.31	21.34	27.30	30.81	33.92	37.66	40.29	48.27
23	10.20	11.29	13.09	14.85	17.19	22.34	28.43	32.01	35.17	38.97	41.64	49.73
24	10.86	11.99	13.85	15.66	18.06	23.34	29.55	33.20	36.42	40.27	42.98	51.18
25	11.52	12.70	14.61	16.47	18.94	24.34	30.68	34.38	37.65	41.57	44.31	52.62
26	12.20	13.41	15.38	17.29	19.82	25.34	31.80	35.56	38.89	42.86	45.64	54.05
27	12.88	14.13	16.15	18.11	20.70	26.34	32.91	36.74	40.11	44.14	46.96	55.48
28	13.57	14.85	16.93	18.94	21.59	27.34	34.03	37.92	41.34	45.42	48.28	56.89
29	14.26	15.57	17.71	19.77	22.48	28.34	35.14	39.09	42.56	46.69	49.59	58.30
30	14.95	16.31	18.49	20.60	23.36	29.34	36.25	40.26	43.77	47.96	50.89	59.70

Distribution of *t*

Degrees of freedom	Probability, P				
	0.1	0.05	0.02	0.01	0.001
1	6.31	12.71	31.82	63.66	636.62
2	2.92	4.30	6.97	9.93	31.60
3	2.35	3.18	4.54	5.84	12.92
4	2.13	2.78	3.75	4.60	8.61
5	2.02	2.57	3.37	4.03	6.87
6	1.94	2.45	3.14	3.71	5.96
7	1.89	2.37	3.00	3.50	5.41
8	1.86	2.31	2.90	3.36	5.04
9	1.83	2.26	2.82	3.25	4.78
10	1.81	2.23	2.76	3.17	4.59
11	1.80	2.20	2.72	3.11	4.44
12	1.78	2.18	2.68	3.06	4.32
13	1.77	2.16	2.65	3.01	4.22
14	1.76	2.14	2.62	2.98	4.14
15	1.75	2.13	2.60	2.95	4.07
16	1.75	2.12	2.58	2.92	4.02
17	1.74	2.11	2.57	2.90	3.97
18	1.73	2.10	2.55	2.88	3.92
19	1.73	2.09	2.54	2.86	3.88
20	1.72	2.09	2.53	2.85	3.85
21	1.72	2.08	2.52	2.83	3.82
22	1.72	2.07	2.51	2.82	3.79
23	1.71	2.07	2.50	2.81	3.77
24	1.71	2.06	2.49	2.80	3.75
25	1.71	2.06	2.49	2.79	3.73
26	1.71	2.06	2.48	2.78	3.71
27	1.70	2.05	2.47	2.77	3.69
28	1.70	2.05	2.47	2.76	3.67
29	1.70	2.05	2.46	2.76	3.66
30	1.70	2.04	2.46	2.75	3.65
40	1.68	2.02	2.42	2.70	3.55
60	1.67	2.00	2.39	2.66	3.46
120	1.66	1.98	2.36	2.62	3.37
Ω	1.65	1.96	2.33	2.58	3.29

These statistical tables are taken from Tables III, p. 46 and IV, p. 47 of Fisher and Yates: *Statistical tables for biological, agricultural and medical research* published by Longman Group Ltd, London (previously published by Oliver and Boyd Ltd, Edinburgh) and by permission of the authors and publishers.

Index

Page numbers in italics refer to text illustrations.